RAISED ON
ELVIS! ELVIS! ELVIS!

RAISED ON ELVIS! ELVIS! ELVIS!

Written by
Sandi Haynes Pichon
&
Thorne Peters

Raised On ELVIS! ELVIS! ELVIS!

Sandi Haynes Pichon
Limited Edition - Copy 767 of 2000

APEX PUBLISHING LTD

First published in 2004 by
Apex Publishing Ltd
PO Box 7086, Clacton on Sea, Essex, CO15 5WN, United Kingdom

Website: www.apexpublishing.co.uk
E-mail: sales@apexpublishing.co.uk

British Library Cataloguing-in-Publication Data
A catalogue record for this book
is available from the British Library

ISBN 1-904444-23-7

Typeset in 10.5pt Baskerville
Production Manager: Chris Cowlin

Cover design by Thorne Peters - www.yoursinelvis.com
Cover created by J. Scott - www.jscottart.com

Printed and bound in Great Britain

Raised On
ELVIS! ELVIS! ELVIS!

a pictorial novella

WRITTEN BY

Sandi Haynes Pichon

Author & President of

TCB ELVIS STYLE FAN CLUB
of Slidell, Louisiana

&

Thorne Peters

Author & President of the

YOURS IN ELVIS FOREVER

Fan Club on ELVIS PRESLEY Blvd.

Dedication by: Kathy Westmoreland

Cover Designed by: Jim Scott of
jscottart.com

PUBLISHED IN THE UNITED KINGDOM BY:
APEX PUBLISHING LTD.

FOREWORD

In August 1970, the very day Elvis finished taping the movie "That's The Way It Is"; I was introduced not only to him, but also to a most baffling world to me - the world of Elvis fans. My first impression was frankly, "This is insanity at it's best!" Men and women getting up on the dinner show tables in Vegas stepping on people's steak dinners, knocking over bottles and glasses of champagne as they ran towards this man attempting to just touch him for a moment, hoping for a kiss, scarf or handshake as he attempted to sing a song. When this scene repeated itself the following night, my first night on stage with him, I trembled with fear! "What's wrong with people?" I thought to myself. I could barely hear my thoughts, much less my voice or Elvis' above the roars of screams coming from these people overwhelmed with adoration and JOY! Yes - Joy - Happiness - at it's most glorious level of demonstration -

was what I had the privilege of witnessing those first few nights... but their excitement frightened me. I truly feared for my life! A few weeks into my adventures with Elvis I began to see and understand what this man did for people. HE MADE THEM HAPPY! If for one night, one hour, in their lives filled with everyday problems, some much more than I could even imagine, they could find a time of happiness, forget their troubles, then this was what it was all about.

As the years went by I, of course, noticed and began to recognize "familiar faces in the crowds. Faithful, loyal fans that did NOT act insane but appeared in certain areas/locations near their homes - within a radius of several states. I now understand - fans that actually appeared to be sane, normal people who just simply loved Elvis and his music. These few not only adored Elvis for the happiness he gave them. But they actually supported and loved each one of us who contributed our tiny part to his shows and records. The very FIRST one of these wonderful people who made ME feel special was Sandi (Hitchcock then) Pichon. Her friend Sue McCasland Olmetti was the other one. Elvis and I thought of them as true FRIENDS and had no fear of talking to them, sharing moments together as normal friends would do at any time they could get together. They never failed to be there when we needed our spirits uplifted. There were so many times Elvis and I said to each other, "What are we doing? What's this all about?" Sandi and her friends were there to remind us that it did have something meaning beyond pure "hysteria".

This book is a TREASURE that reveals the trust about what Elvis meant to his fans. It is written from a sane fan's point of view and her experiences. Most important to me is the fact that she recalls events that even I had forgotten in the midst of living the experience. She also documents and proves what I have been desperately attempting to tell people - that there is a degree of TRUTH that is totally MISSING from all other accounts of Elvis' life, his illnesses being the most important to me. Sandi witnessed first hand the fact that he was NOT just FAT, but that one night he was BLOATED (due to congestive heart disease that he was born with, and not just overeating as had been reported by those who worked for/with him but had no personal knowledge of what really was going on)... and the very next night once the water retention had been controlled, he was totally thin and looked normal again. As one heart surgeon who had been consulted told me, "He was born a dying man. Even if he had lived in a glass bubble, lived the most perfect life as a human being could live, he MAY have lived two weeks longer." To this very day, in the year 2003, there is NOTHING that could be done for one who had his condition. His heart was twice the size on one side as the other. He had inherited this from his mother, her father and her father's brothers, etc. His father, Vernon, also had heart disease. Elvis got it from both sides of the family. Elvis' twin brother, Jesse, died at birth from this defect. Others in his family who lived, all dies in their 40's.

When I first got to know Elvis as a friend, he told me, "I know exactly how much time I have... my mother died at 42 and I will die at 42. I live to make people happy, and I will never stop until the day I die." His mother it seems actually died at 44, but Elvis repeated this to me so many times that I wonder to this day why he said or believed it. Was he just psychic? Is there an historical error regarding his mother's age? I don't know. He also told me that he had a "cancer-like condition" and it turned out he had bone cancer, which had literally riddled his entire body. Other painful diseases he suffered were glaucoma, a twisted colon and conditions that he suffered from birth such as "clinical insomnia". I have been told that many geniuses suffer from this disease - the mind just won't rest. He and his father, Vernon, were known to sleepwalk from their early childhood days. Yes, he and his doctors attempted to control these conditions (high blood pressure being one) with medications that Elvis would abuse on occasions. Contrary to popular history, he was NOT a depressed, miserable rich man who sought to escape his reality with drugs but was truly the happiest rich man I ever knew. He totally trusted his doctors (actually wanted to BE a doctor), believed God worked through them to heal us with their knowledge and skills, and would take more than was prescribed on occasion. Remember, THERE WERE NO "BETTY FORD CLINICS" in those days, and not one of us, not even the doctors themselves, realized the dangers in prescribed medications! His brief episodes of depression overwhelmed him as it would any of us when we are sick and just can't fix our diseases.

It is my honor and privilege to introduce this book to the world and I am certain that most true Elvis fans will completely feel it expresses what they themselves felt and continue to feel today about this great human being and his contribution to the world. I will be forever grateful to my days with Elvis not only for his friendship but also for the TRUE FRIENDSHIP that lasted beyond Elvis' days here on earth. (OOHH - how many so-called "friends" I had when he was alive, who all disappeared that fateful day of August 16, 1977.) It is my sincere hope that even those few, VERY FEW, who weren't fans will actually now have the opportunity to attain a greater understanding of this most precious person who changed even their lives without even knowing it.

Now it is time for you to relax, sit back and READ. Enjoy this gem... this most wonderful book. Thank you, Sandi, for writing this... and thank you for BEING a true friend to

Elvis and to me... and to the others who had the most awesome experience of our lifetimes. THANK YOU.

- **Kathy Westmoreland, 20 February 2003**

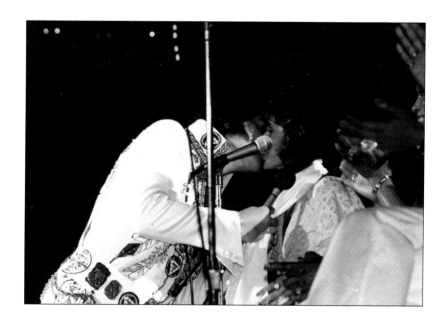

This book is dedicated to the memory of that magical time when Elvis ruled the music world and our hearts, and the legacy he left behind.
The memories of Elvis and his men who have now joined him: Felton, Ed, J.D., Mike, Harold, Vester and Vernon, all so important to Elvis and our world. A man who changed not only the music industry but the world. A man who needs no explanation or introduction -
ELVIS says it all.

I would like to thank the following people for making this book a reality. Kathy Westmoreland, Joyce Hulsey, George Hill, Sean Shaver, Keith Alverson and Kathie Lusch. I would also like to thank James and Carol Light of Memories of Elvis who told me I owed it to the fans to share my memories and pictures.
Special thanks to Keith Alverson for his pictures of Kathy Westmoreland and Elvis which were included in the foreward.

Special thanks to my good friend Pete Smith, "Apache Elvis" who believed in me, encouraged me and worked with me to make this a reality.

I would also like to express my appreciation to the creative talents of Thorne Peters who worked so hard in bringing my story to life and for his constant encouragement and friendship. His talent and hard work will never be forgotten.

And to my husband Stanley, without whose love and support I could never have undertaken this project.

I am writing this book for two reason. As time passes, memories become clouded and some things seem to disappear. This book will always keep the memories of a special time in my life fresh and alive. It also allows me to try and put into perspective the effect Elvis Aron Presley had on my life as well as the effect success had on his. If you are looking for sensationalism, then lay this book aside. This is a reflection on the man caught up in a magical transformation. A man who was placed on a pedestal by millions of people around the world, who refused to let him fall. A man who was loved for his goodness, kindness and the joy he brought others by his God-given talent. A step back in time reliving those wonderful concerts, the excitement and youth of us all.

1956 was a very special year for Elvis Aron Presley

January 22   - Recorded Heartbreak Hotel/I Was the One

January 26   - Appeared on the Dorsey TV show

April   - Played Vegas and bombed, but met Liberace
              - who advised him to "jazz up" his wardrobe

April 3   - Appeared on Milton Berle TV show

April 7   - Signed Paramount Movie Contract

June 28   - Steve Allen Show & Rehearsal in New York

June 30   - Two shows in Richmond, Virginia

July 4   - Russ Wood Stadium, Memphis

August   - Began shooting first movie "Love Me Tender"

September 9   - Appeared on Ed Sullivan Show

September 26 - Tupelo, MS State Fair

November 16   - "Love Me Tender" movie released

In 1956, Elvis became a millionaire. And, he got to meet me, Sandi Haynes Pichon.

THE GREEN GREEN GRASS OF HOME

I was born in Memphis, on October 3, 1944, but when I was just a year old we moved north of Memphis to Tiptonville, the hometown of Carl Perkins. My daddy, J.C Haynes, opened Haynes Cafe there and also served two terms as the Lake County Sheriff. While we were there, my brother, Tim, was born. After getting his fill of politics, my daddy decided to try his hand at farming, so we moved to Gleason, Tennessee, way out in the sticks. My mother, Maxine, was not cutout to be a country girl. As she used to say, "I like bright lights and city sidewalks." The country offered her none of that and more. She hated the farm; she worked like a slave picking and canning peas and beans, and churning butter - she did not find the work rewarding. One day my daddy had gone to take some cattle to auction and a fox was coming down to get into the chicken yard, so she got out the rifle and shot the fox dead. She was a fiercely protective mother that raised us with manners and elegance. On Sundays she set our table with sterling silverware, crystal glasses, fine china, and linen napkins; she poured water from a sterling silver pitcher, and we drank from the matching goblets and now my brother owns the goblets and I own the pitcher.

Tim and I loved living on the farm; we rode horses, walked in the woods, and drank from a babbling brook where clean spring water flowed. We had all kinds of pets - cats, dogs, and a goat; there was even a pond for fishing... it was a great way of life for us kids. But then a terrible accident changed everything. When my brother was in the first grade he was run over by our sharecropper. Tim was riding on the bumper of a John Deere tractor when he fell off of the fender. By some miracle he lived, but it was touch and go for a while. Because of this and my mother's feelings about country life, along with Eisenhower costing the farmers so much money, she wanted to move back to the city. My daddy had to go along with her, and, in early 1956, we returned to the city of my birth, Memphis.

My life on the farm had been educational in many ways, but had been lacking in the ways of social and cultural trends. Moving to Memphis opened my eyes to a whole new world of options; there were so many places to go, so many different things to see and I was eager to do everything. We used to go and eat at the Gayosa Hotel in Memphis and dress to the teeth; I really enjoyed the sophisticated atmosphere. While attending White Station Elementary School in the 6th grade, I went to my first dance. Never mind that I didn't know how to dance, I was determined to go just so I could be a part of the festivities. I held hands with a boy named Welch Agnew and stumbled around the floor with him as best I could. I wasn't going to win any prizes at it, but I sure took to dancing right off. My friend, Rachel, knew how to dance real good, her mom used to waltz us around the floor showing us how to follow and not lead - it was the best kind of fun I knew of. In fact it was at that very dance social that I first heard the name and music of ELVIS PRESLEY.

Music has always been a part of my life. My grandmother, Bernice Foster, worked for radio station WREC based in Memphis, so that's where we stay tuned, except on Saturday nights when The Grand Ole Opry was on. My background and upbringing in music had been Country & Western, even before they called it that, so my favorite performers were Teresa Brewer, Kay Starr, and Gene Austin. I also liked a lot of the other acts on the Hillbilly jamborees. But Memphis was the birthplace of the Rhythm & Blues craze that had taken hold and changed the sound of the national music scene in just a year, so all the kids were listening to Dewey Phillips on WHBQ. His show, "Red, Hot and Blue," had been the top broadcast in the region ever since a hot July night in 1954, when he played a cut by an unknown local truck driver that turned the city on its ear and would later become known as, "The Song That Changed The World."

The country and the world may have been just finding out about Elvis in 1956, but in Memphis and the Mid-South he reigned supreme on the stages for two years and was already a cult legend for the show-stopping riots his performances created. If ELVIS was everywhere, he was the biggest thing in Memphis for sure. This is where his star rose; the onetime high school outcast was now the toast of the town and loved by all. It seemed that most everyone had an Elvis story, about knowing him or his folks or seeing him around or knowing someone who knew him. It wasn't a total love fest, because there were plenty of folks that didn't want their kids listening to his kind of jungle music or watching him on television doing his dirty dancing. It was the "Big Bang" of Rock & Roll and it was an explosion that created the generation gap between adults and children. Parents wanted us kids to like the young, handsome and talented Pat Boone, who was as clean cut and wholesome as milk and cookies. I even remember there was some sort of contest between Elvis and Pat Boone at school, but it was no contest at all; we liked Pat Boone, but we loved Elvis.

"Heartbreak Hotel" raced up the charts in no time and hit Number One. My favorite song was actually the flipside, "I Was The One," and it went to the Number One spot just as soon as "Heartbreak Hotel" moved down. My friends in Memphis knew a lot more about Elvis than I did. I had no idea he had other songs out, because he was new to me like he was most of the country at that time. I loved those exciting records he made at Sun Studios too, and I became a dyed in the wool Elvis fan for life.

Many of these new experiences in some ways were like my preparation for being immersed in Elvis world. I met my first set of twins, Vicki and Valerie Webster, who were Mormon - another first for me. I always thought that twins were supposed to be identical, but the Webster girls were each beautiful in opposite ways. It always made me wonder how opposite or similar Elvis and Jesse might have been. I also had a friend, Gail Perlberg, who was Jewish and lived in the most gorgeous modern house I had ever seen. I never knew anyone who wasn't Protestant before moving to Memphis. Susie Aviazan, was from Paris and she taught me to ask for her in French when I called, because her mother didn't speak any English. Along with my friend, Linda McCree, we all got together and formed "The Busy Bee Club." We met after school at each other's houses to talk about fashions, play records and read about Elvis in fan magazines - practically a training ground for my years as a fan club president.

I had absolutely no sense of style in clothes and didn't know enough to know the difference. I had always liked whatever my mother picked out for me, without realizing her fashion sense was a generation behind the times. However, once I started hanging out at The Drug Store, my teenage friends pointed out that my shorts were too baggy, my skirts were too long, and my outfits were out of date, so I started to pay more attention to how I dressed. I made a new friend, Billie Frances Hall, the daughter of one of my daddy's co-workers who lived nearby. She loved Elvis too and we became fast friends. She was kind of in the know about fashionable trends and in spots and I learned a lot from her. I started listening to the "DJGK Show," on WHBQ, with her, which was hosted by disc jockey George Klein. I got real interested in him especially, because he had gone to school with Elvis and they were friends-I knew this because GK would happen to mention it every few songs... You could dance in the studio during his show, so now and then we caught the bus and spent the afternoon bopping to records from the hit parade.

There was so much to enjoy and I was taking to it all. Memphis offered the Cotton Carnival, an event filled with excitement and the opportunity to dress up - I borrowed my first long dress from my cousin Sylvia for the event. There was the Rainbow Skating Rink, Clearwater Pool, Libertyland, and concerts allover town. Experiencing diverse cultures, styles, theosophies, genetics, social-izing, fashions, dancing, languages, cuisines, and music were giving me a well-rounded outlook and I felt like I was ready for anything.

At this time the music world was all a jumble, between Hillbilly, C&W, R&B and the birth of Rock & Roll. Because of the blending genres, you started seeing all different kinds of artists singing on the same program and it was an exciting format. For instance, on the first weekend in June, we attended a concert at the Overton

Park Shell, which featured Warren Smith, Eddie Bond, Carl Perkins, Roy Orbison, The Teen Kings, and Johnny Cash. I was looking forward to this because I remembered Carl Perkins from Tiptonville. He and his family had entertained at the minstrels held at the local high school, and I wanted to see him again. (I feel that Carl Perkins never got the recognition he deserved for his talent and contribution to the emerging music scene.)

The only thing that would have been even more perfect that day was if Elvis was going to perform, but with all the fine acts there we knew that we were going to see a great show and we were really excited about going. We were on the fourth row, right in the center, so we had a great view. (Little did I know that this close proximity to the stage had already made an impression on my young brain and I would never settle for less!) With autograph books in hand, we worked our way down near the front of the stage to be as much a part of it all as we could. As Warren Smith sang, "Rock & Roll Ruby," my roving eyes caught a flurry of activity backstage. The Shell is an outdoor amphitheater, with rows of bench seats, and there were a lot of people milling around, so it was hard to pick out individuals, but a familiar face caught my eye and I felt my stomach do a flip-flop. I punched Billie Frances to get her attention off of Warren Smith, because I was sure that I had seen Elvis! She thought I was going crazy, but suddenly there he was on stage, a surprise walk-on guest, introduced by the emcee as, "A successful local boy with a Number One hit!"

We burst into frantic screams at the sight of Elvis standing before us. He smiled casually, but appeared a little nervous at the pandemonium he created. I wasn't doing anything more than staring at him, because I couldn't move. He didn't seem like he was a real everyday person; there was something about him that defied description. He was wearing a white sport coat with stripes of green, black and gold. His smile was gleaming, his hair was glistening, and he was bathed in a visible aura. He seemed to be waving right at me in the crowd and, just as I raised my arm to wave back, a photographer from the Commercial Appeal snapped a picture of us. The next day there I was, front page of the second section; my autograph book in the hand of my outstretched arm reaching for the impossible dream. I wouldn't know it until years later, but at that moment we had bonded the very nature of our relationship for life.

Elvis didn't sing that night, but his appearance whetted our appetites for more. After the show we met all the singers and they signed my autograph book, which became my prized possession. I was overjoyed to have been part of this magical moment, but oh how I wished that I could have gotten Elvis to write his name in my book.

THIS IS ELVIS!

We heard Elvis would be appearing at Russwood Park for a July 4 celebration, so we begged our parents for tickets and a ride there. It was a traditionally sweltering evening, which heightened the frenzy of the restless crowd of tens of thousands of teens who were chanting, "ELVIS! ELVIS! ELVIS!" long before the show was scheduled to begin. There were other entertainers - I remember a Navy band, of all things (maybe they had followed Elvis from the "Milton Berle Show" when Elvis sang aboard the aircraft carrier U.S.S Hancock) - but my memory of who the acts were or what they did was obliterated by the performance of the headlining showstopper. This was my first Elvis concert and I tried to savor every moment, so that I could create a time capsule in my mind. We saw twin girls who had personalized their outfits; E-L-V-I-S was spelled in bright pink letters down the legs of their black pants. Pink and black were rumored to be his favorite colors at that time and we all got caught up in that trend. Boys our age were already copying his hairstyle; even though they were too young for sideburns, they had combed their long hair into the cascading style in front, called a "Balboa," with the "DA" in back. The stage was set up outside, fairground style, and the crowds were standing, not seated. Colonel Parker's presence could be felt everywhere, as all through the crowd vendors were selling every imaginable souvenir with Elvis' name and likeness on it. We had gotten there while it was still daylight and by 10 p.m. we wanted Elvis more than ever! After a veritable cavalcade of carny acts and vaudeville performances, the restless crowd was getting hysterical! It went on so long that I started thinking that he was never going to come out... but then there he was...

There were no kettledrums to herald his arrival, just the screams of the girls who saw him first as he strutted toward the microphone with his guitar slung around on his back and a mischievous gleam in his eyes. We were very near the stage and I had to step back, as best I could, to get a better look, by craning my neck around the people in front of me. Suddenly he was center stage, right before my very eyes, dressed in all black except for a bright red tie. He held his pose for a moment to absorb the crowd's adulation then erupted into the song that had gotten him started on the road to the top, just a day shy of two years before.

If just seeing him standing on a stage smiling and waving had such a dramatic effect on me when we were at the Shell, witnessing him here in all his glory, unleashing his passionate persona through his music and gyrations was overwhelming. I wasn't aware that a lump had formed in my throat or that tears were streaming down my cheeks; it was a strange reaction to have to something that you were enjoying, but I wasn't the only one dissolving in tears. I was having an out of body experience, because I felt like I was up there with him. I stood there, looking up at this boy/man and felt as though something incredible was happening to me. I couldn't explain it to someone, even if they had seen him, because everyone had their own feelings about what Elvis did to them inside.

I tried to take it all in. Elvis was sly and witty when he set up songs. For instance he announced, "This next song, friends, is plum pitiful. It's a little number called, 'Get Outta The Barn, Grandma; You're Too Old To Be Horsing Around!'" He spoke to the audience in a breathy voice, grunting and stammering and panting; he flirted and leered, and the girls responded by rushing up to get a kiss or a touch from him. He dramatically wailed and crooned while rolling allover the stage, which really whipped up the crowd. Elvis teased the audience into a heightened state of exhilaration and it kept the security guards on their toes, because so many Elvis concerts had turned into madhouses. He was in a rare form this night; it was obvious. The guys behind him kicked up quite a ruckus on their instruments and Elvis reacted with his wild pelvic dances and wiggling legs as he went from one end of the stage to the other leaving girls screaming and fainting allover the place in his wake.

What I didn't know then was that Elvis was going the extra mile at this show. Only days before he had been set up to play the fool on "The Steve Allen Show," when he was dressed in a tux and made to sing to a hound dog while standing nearly still. Elvis smiled and took it all in good fun publicly, but behind the scenes he seethed over being humiliated like that in front of a national audience. From the stage that night he announced with conviction to his hometown fans, "Don't y'all worry about a thing, friends; them folks up North ain't gonna change me none! Tonight I'm gonna show you the real Elvis Presley in action!"... he proceeded to rip it up like never before...

I was right there, watching every move he made, laughing at all the jokes he cracked, and going wild before, during and after each song. I was so fascinated by his mannerisms; the way he hitched his shoulders, the stiff way he held his fingers, the way he'd flare his nostrils and snarl as he smiled, the wild-eyed way he'd raise his eyebrows when he'd launch into one of his dance numbers during the guitar solos, the way that he played around with his guys on stage, was all so captivating. I couldn't figure out how he could chew gum and sing like he did. I was close enough that I could hear him quite clearly in spite of the screams and applause that went on right through his performance. At times it was as though I was the only person in the audience. At one point I was certain that he caught my eye and winked right at me, but then I'm sure every girl standing in that area thought the same thing - maybe all of us were right to think that. Billie Frances had this glazed look in her eyes and we were speechless, so we just stared blankly at each other now and then - we couldn't believe our eyes or ears. It was one of those night-of-nights that comes once in a lifetime - even though I would later have many encores of nights like this, this was the encounter that touched my life most deeply, because I was so young and vulnerable and filled with such high hopes for the future... so was Elvis...

I don't remember the show ending or even going home; all I know is that I woke up the next morning still not understanding what I had experienced. Billie Frances came over later, and we tried to explain what we had experienced, but we didn't have a clue... there were no words... we just knew that we had to do all that we could do to see him every chance that we could... and we did.

During the summer we caught the bus and rode downtown to Wink Martindale's "Dance Party," as well as the "DJGK Show," as often as we could. Both of these shows were so much fun; we danced - sometimes with each other and sometimes with boys - and talked to anybody we could find that had any connection with Elvis. We watched George Klein through the glass booth and he would wink at us and smile; he was very personable. The best thing about Memphis was that there were a lot of outdoor shows in parks, and it didn't cost a lot to go, so it was a great way to spend a day. Times sure have changed, because I couldn't imagine letting an 11-year-old out to go to a concert on their own in a big city, but that was the way of things then - the world was a safer place for children.

I cannot remember the exact date or day of the week, but it was right after I turned 12 that October - it was still hot enough to feel like summer, but that's Memphis most of the time. We were kicking around with nothing to do and got bored. We had been over to the drug store, but none of our crowd was there. I had walked through the Big Star Supermarket gaping at Jerry Houston, a 9th grader who didn't even know I existed, so that was uneventful. I guess that the more bored you get, the more desperate you get to do something exciting. I must've been mighty bored, because I suddenly just blurted out, "Hey, let's go over to Elvis' house!" Billie Frances was stunned by my idea and didn't respond. Without waiting for her to answer, I ran inside and asked my mother if she would pretty please - take us to Elvis' place. We could've walked, because it wasn't that far, but it was too darn hot, so I wheedled my mother to take us over just for a bit. Being a great mother, she always did what she could to support my fancies, so she agreed and we were off to see the king of our hearts.

As we neared 1034 Audubon Drive I asked her to pull over to the curb and let us out - after all, I didn't want Elvis to see my mother bringing us! I had just turned 12, so I didn't want him to think that I was some baby. She was an understanding good sport about these things, so she let us out up the block and sat there in the car waiting for us in that miserable Memphis heat.

Billie Frances and I marched up to the back door (because in the South, the front door is for company) and knocked. The maid answered and when we asked for Elvis she said that he was sleeping. Sleeping, at 4:00 o'clock in the afternoon? "We'll wait," I announced. There was a yellow Cadillac convertible in the driveway as well as a green motorcycle next to the house under the carport. Billie Frances jumped onto the right fender of the car and I hopped up and straddled the motorcycle. We talked excitedly, wondering if he would actually come out and what we'd do if he did. I looked around the grounds and saw some construction going on in the backyard where a swimming pool was being dug and an enclosed garage was being built. Then a pink Cadillac drove up and parked on the left side of the yellow Cadillac. It was Elvis' parents returning from the grocery store. They both greeted us politely; Mrs. Presley offered us a glass of lemonade, which we eagerly accepted. Mr. Presley carried in a watermelon and when he returned to get the rest of the groceries, he brought us the lemonade.

We continued to wait patiently, but as time passed by it seemed less and less likely that we would get our chance to meet with Elvis. I would have waited there forever, if I had to, or at least all night, but I knew that my mother was trapped down the street roasting in our car and I started thinking that we would have to give up our quest... at least for that day... I was looking ahead when suddenly I felt these arms go around me from behind and a voice ask, "Wanna go for a ride?" It was Elvis and he was sitting on his motorcycle with me! I promptly spilled the rest of my lemonade and just froze. He inquired, "What can I do for you girls?" I heard Billie Frances saying that we wanted an autograph, but I really couldn't focus, because I was so lightheaded. He laughed right next to my ear; I could feel his cool breath against my hair; I had shivers and goose bumps! Finally I was able to turnaround and look into the handsomest face and bluest eyes of anyone ever and a part of my heart was pledged to him eternally right in that one moment.

When he got off of the motorcycle, we produced our autograph books and hovered as close to him as we could while he signed. We were so entranced that when he asked us our names, we had to look at each other and get our bearings before we could answer - he chuckled at our hesitation, probably because it happened all the time. I had a long moment to take him in from head to toe and I did. Even though it was as hot as Memphis, he had on a long sleeved, green shirt that had black laces at the neck hanging loose. He was sporting a black motorcycle cap that he wore cocked to one side. With all the grace of a 12-year-old I tried to mumble something reasonably intelligent, but no words came out that I could understand. He was real natural and relaxed in his way, but we were so in awe of him that we just giggled and babbled. He handed back the book and it read, "To Sandra, Love, Elvis Presley" LOVE! This was before the world had cast its shadow on Elvis and he could write, "Love." In later years a woman in Florida filed a paternity suit against him and offered as proof a picture he had signed "With Love." After that, he quit signing "Love," but it was always in his heart for his fans.

On this momentous day in 1956, Elvis Presley told us to come back anytime we wanted to then climbed onto his motorcycle and roared off into the sunset alone. Not quite ready to leave, I really wanted to get inside, so I knocked on the door and asked if I could use the phone to call someone to come and get us, even though my mother was stewing in the car just down the block. I was admitted to the kitchen and I started looking around at as much of everything as I could. I had never seen so many kinds of different appliances as there were in that kitchen. The walls were all done in bright patterns with dark paneling, and there was a breakfast nook, which curved around the corner. I made my bogus phone call, said my thank-yous and left. Well you can bet we were floating on air after that and I didn't mind showing off my autograph to anyone who wanted a look - and everyone did.

Taking Elvis at his word, we went back to his house several times in the upcoming weeks. I think that Mr. & Mrs. Presley, George Klein, and Red West just tolerated us as local kids and let us hang out, for a short time, but Elvis was sweet and would spare a minute if he had it. I could never have looked ahead and realized how important those memories would become. I took so much for granted; I thought that I would get to visit Elvis forever! So many hundreds of times I've wondered why I never thought to ask my parents to buy a camera, so I could have made a visual record of our moments in the sun all those years ago.

Even though I was on the fringe looking in, I was part of Elvis' world and got to hear about some of the happenings firsthand. Right about then his neighbors on Audubon Drive were complaining all the time about him - everything from the way his fans drove by and congregated at all hours to his momma hanging out her laundry on a clothesline in the backyard. The neighbors got together and offered to buy Elvis' home, so Elvis countered by offering to buy up all of their homes then reminded them that he had the only house on the block that was paid in full!

My parents laughed at the stories of intrigue I told them. They thought Elvis was a neat guy and I was glad they liked him. They didn't have a problem with me spending my free time hanging around Elvis' house, which is where I would've kept on going for the rest of my life if I had my way about it. Unfortunately this dreamy world was shattered when once again my father got the wanderlust and decided to move us to Florida. It would be another 16 years before I saw Elvis again. By then we had come a far piece from those carefree days of youthful invincibility and were heading down paths that we could have never imagined traveling on during that era of innocence.

DON'T LEAVE ME NOW!

Every time I thought of Memphis, I thought of Elvis and I could feel his arms around me... I guess that's why I always get a tender feeling when I think of Memphis to this very day - some moments really can last a lifetime. As I went through adolescence, I kept up with Elvis in the papers and from friends in the Memphis area - those gossipy teen mags and Hollywood scandal sheets worked overtime to keep you up on what El was doing. Not long after I left, Elvis moved away from Audubon Drive, and bought a big country estate outside Memphis that even came with a name - Graceland. I was glad for his success, but I was sad that he wouldn't be living at the Audubon Drive house anymore... but then I couldn't wait to see his Graceland Mansion. If ever I got back to Memphis I'd just go up to the gates and announce that I was there to see Elvis; after all, I still had a standing invitation from him to come by anytime and I might just try to use it.

Even though Elvis was far away, he was close at hand; his records played everywhere and he made movies one right after another. I was pretty sure that no one else in the theater audience had ever seen him singing right to them or sat on his motorcycle in his front yard drinking a glass of lemonade made by his momma and served to me by his daddy and it made me feel special. If someone didn't believe that I had once been associated with Elvis and his guys, why I'd whip out my autograph book and they'd just stare with envy at the greatest name in all the wide world. Unfortunately that's how my book ended up being stolen. I knew the two girls that did it, but since I couldn't prove it I was never able to recover it. There were so many priceless autographs in there and one that I treasured above all the others... I'm still heartsick over it...

I bought every magazine or newspaper with an Elvis story. I would read every line of the article until I had absorbed it for life then cutout the pictures of him (making sure to cutaway any girl

15

that might be in the picture) and covered every inch of the walls and ceiling of my room - it wouldn't be the last room I'd do that to. My parents owned the Mayfair Drive - in the restaurant right across from our home, and my mother would send people over to go see my "Elvis Room." In my world I was the leading representative and the final authority on Elvis and I was sort of well known in our circle as "The Elvis-girl." I loved it! Everywhere I went I wore a black sailor hat that had "ELVIS" stitched across the side in pink lettering. Then one day at a department store in the South Gate Mall, I saw a black motorcycle hat with a star on it that was nearly identical to the one Elvis was wearing when we met - every time I put it on I was back sitting on that motorcycle with Elvis in my heart and mind.

I kept hoping that he'd come play down in Florida. In 1956 a Jacksonville juvenile court issued a restraining order against his pelvis and filmed the show, so Elvis only used hand gestures, pinky waves and suggestive looks to drive the audience crazy - he probably wasn't anxious for a return engagement. Actually Elvis was phasing out concert performances after relentlessly touring for three years. It seemed odd that he wasn't performing as much, because the whole mystique of the Elvis legend came from the bewitching effect he had on live audiences of flesh and blood females who would chase him off the stage so they could strip his clothes right off his back - even though Elvis was a very fast runner, they'd always manage to catch him somehow... Often he'd do a concert in the day, one in the evening somewhere else then head for one of the coasts to do a television show, or make a movie, or both. Then it was back to Nashville to make records - he recorded in Nashville instead of Memphis, to be closer to New York and the East coast concert markets. He even made it as far as Canada, but had not put together the tour of Europe that he wanted to do so very much. Elvis was the most popular individual on the face of the earth and everyone wanted him everywhere, but he was only one man and he could only go so far.

His hectic schedule was taking its toll on his young constitution. Every now and then Elvis would collapse from exhaustion and be rushed to the hospital. We'd read about him resting comfortably then breathe a sigh of relief that our hero was going to be all right. He had gone further than anyone had in the annals of Pop Culture; he was Number One in the record business, Number One in the movie industry, top of the charts on the radio, lord of the jukebox, and the greatest live performer in the history of entertainment; he was such a megastar that his persona could be seen universally by the naked eye and he was on a first name basis with the world... by the time he turned 23 years old, he had lived a lifetime and was in need of a long rest.

He was about to start making his fourth motion picture in a - year-and-a-half... a thrilling musical drama, based on a best selling Harold Robbins novel that was going to be filmed on location in New Orleans. The press reported how excited he was to do this movie, because James Dean was to have starred in it had he lived. Dean was Elvis' hero, so I was very happy for his success.

Then out of the blue came the announcement that Elvis was being drafted. It really shouldn't have been a shock, because that was the way of things for men in those days. But when it was announced that he'd be going overseas to Germany, rumors and theories sprang up everywhere. Some said that he was being abducted by the Army as part of a government conspiracy to have him killed by the commies, so that we'd have a reason to drop the bomb on Russia. Everyone had an opinion, but almost no one believed that he got drafted and sent to Germany just because his number came up and that's where he was assigned. Looking back it seems that there may have been some truth to some of this speculation, because the powers - that - be took the highest paying individual taxpayer in the country and really shipped him off as close to Siberia as they could. It was the frontlines of the Cold War and, if World War III had started, Elvis would have been among the first to perish. It was the height of the Nuclear Age when we had drop drills in school telling us what to do if and when the Russians dropped the bomb on us, so the threat was very real and a generation of kids were very worried about Elvis.

By then Elvis was no longer in competition with Pat Boone for top spots on the Pop Charts; he was competing against President Eisenhower for domination of the 1950s. (Presley For Prexy!) The only political endorsement Elvis ever gave was for Adilai Stevenson. It was, "I Like Ike," v.s "We Love ELVIS! ELVIS! ELVIS!" Eisenhower may have had peace of mind for the second half of his last term of office with Elvis stashed on another continent, hip deep in snow, standing gun to gun with the Red Army, as the scout of General Patton's old tank brigade, but Elvis had already captured the era. He was a one-man cultural, revolution that changed the way a generation saw itself; he showed us that we could have a say in the way of things. We were the first generation of empowered youth with a disposable income that built empires - soft drinks, fast food, novelty items, and Rock & Roll records. When the teens and teenyboppers came of voting age several years later they responded to Kennedy's idealistic platitudes, because they had seen the "American Dream" come true, with Elvis. Adults historically cast their votes for the present, while youth votes for the future. Without the trailblazing path that Elvis forged, young people would have voted along the party line with their parents, as ever, and not nearly as many women and Blacks would have voted, so Kennedy would have never become President, no matter how many votes his father bought. For this and more a panel of world historians from the A&E Channel chose Elvis as one of the "100 Most Influential People of the Millennium" - Eisenhower and Kennedy did not make the list.

His induction was covered from the head of his G.I hair to the heels of his G.I. shoes, as they snapped pictures and filmed every inch of him that they could during his indoctrination into the Army. They ran the pictures and stories on Page One and in centerfold exclusives and in dramatized teen magazine features; it was covered on the nightly newscasts on television and in Movietone Newsreels at the theater. There were girls around the world threatening to kill themselves, if Elvis was sentenced to two years in the Army - some were going to throw themselves onto the tracks in front of the train taking him away, as a sacrifice to their deity... with something like that it's the thought that counts and thank

God nobody was harmed by their overwrought sentiments... however some women did throw their clothing or lift up their dresses for his benefit along the train route and the shocking behavior of his fans added to his controversial legend.

He was getting through boot camp when his momma got sick and died without any warning; she was just 46 years old and only starting to live the good life he had always wanted to give her. The papers spared no ink on covering his grief and used long lenses to capture private moments for their photo spreads. I was sad that he wasn't allowed to mourn for her in peace. I had a vision of that sweet cherubic woman with the down-home manners and kindly way and I cried for her. How goodhearted she was to worry that a couple of trespassing young girls might need some lemonade in that heat. She had instilled in Elvis her strong sense of consideration for others and it was the part of himself he was the most proud of, because it reflected well on her. She was as precious a woman as Elvis always said she was and he never ever got over her death, because they shared the same spirit. If not for her absolute belief in his vision of himself, the world would never have gotten to know her amazing son.

While in Germany there were magazine pictures of him in uniform carrying a gun or riding in a tank; there were cutout Elvis dolls in Army outfits, and dog tags like his you could buy. The Colonel wasn't going to miss out on any opportunity to market his boy and he masterminded the greatest trinket souvenir market ever seen... of course selling Elvis merchandise is about as difficult as selling water in the desert. The Colonel put together all these golden compilation albums and re-released repackaged albums and singles. Just before shipping out, Elvis got a 3-day pass and went to Nashville for a farewell recording date, so he could stay on the charts after he was long gone - but he hoped not forgotten. While wearing his uniform, he recorded, "Fool Such As I," and "Wear My Ring Around Your Neck." Both were big hits and upbeat tunes, but I got sad hearing them, because the words he sang sounded like he was saying goodbye to us forever. Elvis was in fact very worried that his career would be over and it stayed on

19

his mind the entire time he was away. I guess you could say that those were his first message songs to his fans... "Pardon me if I'm sentimental when we say goodbye"... "When you're gone I'll dream a little dream as years go by." He was telling us how much he was going to miss us. He taught us how to love and even if we were through with him he'd love us till the day he died. Then he asked us to wear his ring around our necks, to let the world know we loved him so. He sounded so vulnerable that I wanted to smother him with hugs!

We were given our first mass death scare when reports flashed around the world that he had been killed in a car wreck. Then we read how the Army would not remove his million dollar tonsils, so he had to suffer through the infection in a hospital bed, while we prayed for his recovery. Just when it seemed that he'd be in the Army forever, he was finally released and headed home to pick up the pieces of his life and careers... for the first time he would have to go it alone, without his momma there as a touchstone to his roots and a guide along the bumpy road ahead.

ELVIS IS BACK!

After two years off of the ever-changing charts, the establishment thought he'd just be a fad from the past that had faded - they figured he'd have to go open a Cadillac dealership in his front yard to make ends meet when he got home. But Elvis ruled and nothing or no one was going to change that. In fact I think his absence did make our hearts grow fonder, because while he was away we rallied as fans and formed a bond with him and each other that could never be broken. Sure, we may have listened to Ricky Nelson, Fabian, Frankie Avalon, and a lot of other conk haired pretty boys that came up and went down, but Elvis was the real deal and no one was going to take his place in our hearts or on the charts - the other guys were just keeping the throne warm for him until he came marching home and went roaring back to the top of the heap. I guess you could say that in many ways those guys were the first Elvis impersonators.

As soon as Elvis was safely home, it seems that the world turned around on me and before I knew it I was a completely different person. I became a rebellious teenager; I still don't know why. At 16 I ran away from a wonderful home to get married and soon my home life was miserable. As time went on, my feelings for Elvis seemed immature and dreamlike - a mere childish fantasy, like wanting to be a fairy princess or a ballerina. So I sat on his motorcycle with him and got a hug; so big deal! So I saw him in concert and he may or may not have winked at only me; so what if he did? None of that had anything to do with the real world of an adult, so why hold onto such silly fancies? I stopped telling anybody about my relationship with Elvis, because I doubted they would've believed me anyway... or cared. With a husband, a job, a baby, chores, and bills, I didn't exactly have time for a hobby.

Soon I rebelled against my love for Elvis like it was a foolish notion and I lost a portion of my soul. I gave away one of my beloved scrapbooks to Rosemary Thompson, a high school classmate. I simply discarded my Elvis hat, necklace, dolls, and t-shirts, as if they were so much junk that was causing clutter in my life and home. Oh how I rue the memory of those days! Fortunately my mother packed away some of my mementos and saved many of my magazines from that era, along with another scrapbook, and my Elvis tennis shoes from 1956 - they've turned yellow! My mother knew that my love for Elvis wasn't just a phase and I would one day realize that. She was always looking out for me; like I said before, she was a great mother!

My adult life was not about enjoying music and dancing; it was about dealing with an abusive husband and coping with being a teen mother. It took me three long years to wise up and move on, but the damage was done and I was at my lowest point ever. I didn't have much to look forward to and I was so young I didn't understand what was happening to me or why or how to make myself feel better; I was depressed but didn't know the meaning of the word so I couldn't name the feelings I sometimes had. I didn't have time to enjoy the beauty of the world, so I just shunned those warm feelings and tender memories. With two jobs, college courses, and a child to raise I had to stay focused on my mind not my heart. Elvis was off living the dream life in mansions from Hollywood to Memphis, making hit records, starring in big box office movies, and dating leading ladies, while I had faced the mundane routine of my everyday life.

However, when my sorrow left me with no place to turn, I instinctively pulled out my Elvis records and it was as if they spoke directly to me. By the time I was 23 I had lived a lifetime, and I was in need of a long rest. I had changed so much that I could hardly connect with the feelings of that little girl of yesteryear. Memphis and Elvis represented the best days of my life, but I couldn't remember the euphoria... the more I listened the more I could feel myself come alive again; I was in touch with myself finally; I reached back to find my heart and the deeper I went the stronger my feelings for Elvis became. It wasn't long before the flood of memories cascaded down to my core and I was overwhelmed. I then scrambled to save every memento of his that I still had left and wept bitterly for those, which were lost to me forever.

Elvis and his career had undergone some drastic changes since I last followed him intently. I guess the biggest news he had made in a while was when it was announced that the world's most eligible bachelor was getting married to the girl he met in Germany that had been rumored to be living at Graceland since she was sweet sixteen - female hearts broke the world over. After a decade of success in Hollywood, his movie format had been worn out and his soundtrack recordings were no longer hits. Slowly but surely Elvis was beginning to fade in popularity and was no longer expanding his fan base. He hadn't been deposed, but he was certainly in exile. The tone of the stories about him had also changed. Instead of talking about how great he was and who he was off dating, they talked about him being washed up and compared him unfavorably to The Beatles. He was no longer in the teen mags; after all he was in his thirties. He was growing more handsome all the time, but wasn't considered a sex symbol anymore. His look was passé in trendy circles compared to the hippy culture that was in style; he had a clean - cut reputation as a wholesome, God-fearing man that never swore, smoke or drank... hardly the image of a Rock star. Getting married didn't make him seem any hipper to the "Now Generation."

Elvis had become the biggest star in the world by bucking the establishment; by then he was the establishment. While The Stones had riots at their concerts, and The Doors caused controversy on television with their lyrics, and The Who trashed hotel rooms, Elvis made family oriented, 40's style MGM musical comedies where he sang to girls and kids and dogs while taking pratfalls. He hadn't performed a concert in eight years and only had a few hits in that time. If anyone wrote something flattering about Elvis it was for who he was before rather than who he was then. When it was announced that he would do a Christmas Special on television everyone thought that it would be the death knell for his career as a relevant artist of his time and from then on he would be a relic of nostalgia.

But the "Singer Special" (later dubbed the "Comeback Special") turned out to be the biggest event in music and proved that Elvis was still Number One. After the show all the women talked about how gorgeous he was in his black leather; men grew their sideburns and wore their collars turned up. He sang all our old favorites, but in a completely different way. He was sensual and powerful and in command, despite being so nervous behind the scenes that he would fail. But Elvis had been in much tougher spots and triumphed, and this show was a monument to his resolve. From the shacks, dumps and projects where he lived to dives and holes in the walls where he played, he had dared to be creative and he thrived beyond his situation. From local then regional then national and finally global fame and fortune, he had risen up to become the most recognized man in the world with a voice that has been heard more than anyone else's. From the cruel children that tormented him for his background and ways to the press that crucified him for his artistic expression, his talent, power, and courage allowed him to persevere and achieve the pinnacle of idolatry. He may have had doubts about his ability to excite the crowd after all those years away, but his fans didn't. It sure felt good telling all of his detractors, "I told you so!"... it still does.

Right after that he was back in concert and fans flew in from around the world to gather at the footlights in awe and amazement. When he went on concert tours, international audiences arranged their vacation time so that they could fly or drive to the U.S cities and towns where he performed. He remains the Number One human tourist attraction in history. Posters of him were everywhere again and he was cutting Top Ten hits. This was a brand new Elvis who was virile and macho - instead of excited screaming girlies out there, the audience was filled with aroused grown women who threw their panties and room keys onto the stage throughout the show. He flirted and teased the audiences with touches and kisses and they responded by tearing at his costume; he loved creating pandemonium by just jumping off the stage to walk through the audience. It was a total love fest that has never ended.

By doing it his way, he again showed his determination to follow his own vision, rather than join the trend. He didn't transform himself into a hippie, the way Bobby Darin and Ricky Nelson tried to do, he didn't do a blast from the past concert tour the way that Jerry Lee Lewis, Chuck Berry, and Little Richard were doing at that time. True to the era, Elvis did his own thing and he did it better than anyone else. While hundreds of thousands were gathering at Woodstock, hundreds of thousands were coming to Las Vegas - another hundred thousand went to the Houston Astrodome. While tens of thousands of Dead Heads hitchhiked and camped out to follow the band around the country, committing crimes along the way, millions from around the world flew to wherever Elvis was and brought a fortune with them. He was one man taking on his industry peer group and he was dominating. His new releases received saturation airplay and sold out in record stores; recordings of his concert performances became big selling hits; his classic cuts received saturation airplay on the Oldies stations and continued selling well in record stores worldwide; his music was also a big favorite on Country stations and on stations in other countries where they don't even speak the language he was singing in.

To top it all off they even made a movie about Elvis in concert, so that we could enjoy a twenty foot tall Elvis in action. It was incredible! The concert footage was breathtaking, but I was touched by the down to earth way he came off in his quiet moments. He had a wonderful rapport with the people around him and you could see how deeply they cared for him; they were awed, but it didn't stop them from making a connection. I liked how Elvis made popular songs over in his own style, just as he had done in the beginning. He worked well with the talented group and was very much in charge. He had put this group together with his heart, and filled it with people that were into playing music the way he wanted to hear it. He brought together fantastic individuals from diverse musical and ethnic backgrounds and blended them into a harmonious group that became part of something so special. They had to be pretty incredible, just to keep up with him.

Feeling better about myself, and my prospects, I decided to let love into my life again and gave marriage another try. Soon after I was living in Atlanta, Georgia. In April 1972, Elvis was appearing in Macon, Georgia and I convinced some friends to go with me. The tickets I was able to get were on the fourth row right in the center! I thought back to that first show at the Shell where I was on the fourth row in the center and smiled to myself. We listened to the corny jokes of Jackie Kahane, which in the coming years I could recite from memory, and then there was an intermission. On my way to get a soft drink I saw Red West standing by the fence that blocked off the backstage area. Just as the lights dimmed, I walked over and he said that I looked familiar. I told him that I was surprised he'd recognize me at all after 16 years, and then I explained how I used to stop by the house on Audubon Drive now and then - one of hundreds undoubtedly. He didn't know my name, so I introduced myself to him. He was polite and said that it was nice seeing me; I was strangely happy after that simple exchange.

I returned to my seat just as the lights went down and the kettledrums began roll. The building horns of "2001: A Space Odyssey," reached a blaring climax then played a heralding refrain, as the band kicked in with the rolling opening riff... Elvis, suddenly appeared and you could feel the impact that his presence had on the audience. Even though you knew he was coming out it was still stunning to see ELVIS there before your very eyes. He was wearing a sparkling white jumpsuit with an ornate cape and he looked quite trim and fit. He strutted across the stage forward and backwards, greeting the audience with nods and smiles and acknowledging his band. He playfully gestured toward his large group of handclapping, harmonizing back up singers then went over to Charlie so he could put a guitar around his neck. They passed a word and a smile then Elvis took center stage and struck a powerful pose, which sent a roar through the crowd. He waited a moment to let the music engulf him then began singing with a voice that was surprisingly rich and powerful

- his voice always sounded incredible on record, but in concert you could feel his performance; it touched you, it moved you, it inspired you.

I could hardly believe this polished entertainer was the same boyish man I had met so many years ago. I was transported back to Russwood Park and experienced that funny feeling in my stomach again. I was lightheaded I had a lump in my throat, moisture in my eyes and goose bumps on my arms before he was through singing, "C.C Rider," and I was even more jittery and altered by the time he closed with, "Can't Help Falling In Love." I guess in some ways I've never been the same since that night... he touched my very soul.

It also brought back memories of the last time I saw him in concert and I naturally drew comparisons. As different as his sound, wardrobe, and presence were, nothing had really changed. I mean Elvis was still E-L-V-I-S. His renowned sideburns were back fuller than ever and his hair was fashionably long. His young and beautiful looks had developed into classic features that were defined and ethereal. The sweet high whine of youth had been honed into a resonant primal wail, but each emanated from his soul. Whether he was gyrating his legs or throwing karate kicks he was still carried across the stage by his flashy moves; he no longer jiggled his pelvis playfully, he thrust it forcefully... it all had the same effect on the audience who screamed like they were on a roller coaster. When he left the stage, cape flaring behind him I felt exhilarated, excited, and all warm inside. I just knew I'd see him again - I just had to! What I didn't know is that he would become part of my everyday life.

It was more than a spectacular concert by the artist of the millennium; it was a touchstone to me. I felt a personal connection to him, which led me back to the comforting days of raw innocence I had known when we were together at his house. It made me think of all the happy hours I spent poring over stories and pictures of him and decorating my room with his countenance. I had come full circle and I was home again in my heart. It had been a long hard road, but somehow I felt that everything was going to be all right; I suddenly looked forward to the future more than ever with total belief that better days were ahead - just like I did when I was a kid.

Then he was off two months to gear up for a weekend at Madison Square Garden that has never been equaled by any artist, combination of groups or sporting events that have played in that historic building. The small town boy had some of his most acclaimed moments in the great metropolis, from his world shaking television appearances to his traffic stopping debut movie premiere - Elvis could make it anywhere!

Al Aronowitz of the New York Post captured the moment and the man like no other when he wrote: "...the moon and the sun are his competition... Elvis opened doors for us that no one else had the strength to, and his lofty position in our history, our everlasting debt to him was scored and locked up long ago. He is so obviously one of the greatest phenomena of our time that he is beyond any kind of criticism... Just to hear him sing is to know he has been touched by the finger of God and to see him sing only multiplies proof... once in a lifetime a special champion comes along someone in whose hands the way a thing is done becomes more important than the thing itself. At Madison Square Garden Elvis was like that. He stood there at the end, a champion. The only one in his class." These lines still are still applicable.

KING OF THE WHOLE WIDE WORLD!

Little did I know that the concert would prove to be the last joyous hour I would know for a longtime to come. The Monday following the concert I was involved in a near-fatal collision on my way to work, which resulted in a lengthy hospital stay. I had to have multiple surgeries and was given a 1 in 20 chance to live. Thanks to the skilled doctors and lots of prayers, I began to heal. However, the strain and stress proved too much for my husband. He was unable to take care of my son, do the laundry and household chores, work all day then come to see me in the hospital, so he farmed my child out to neighbors and stayed away as much as he could. I spent many hours alone and lonely, just sitting in my hospital room listening to Elvis songs on my son's record player.

Out of sheer boredom one day I decided to write Elvis a letter, never expecting a reply. It was cathartic I guess, because I wanted to relive a happier time. I told him of how we met those many years ago and how thrilled I was to have seen him in concert then and now. Just mailing it off made me excited, so you can imagine my surprise when two weeks later the lady who brought the mail came into my room and said, "You have a letter from Elvis Presley!" I beamed with joy as she handed me the manila envelope then stood by eagerly as I opened it. Inside was a letter from Elvis' office wishing me a speedy recovery and there was an autographed promotional picture enclosed. It was an artist's drawing of him in a white jumpsuit with a red belt. It had been signed before the print was made, but above the printed signature it was signed again, "To Sandra, Best Wishes, Elvis Presley." No, "Love Elvis," but that was okay. It suited me just fine to have received anything, let alone something so personalized. I was certain that he had no idea who I was and doubted that he read my letter, but having that picture of him perked me up and made me feel closer to him.

Once I got home to begin my recuperation, I learned through

Jim Howell, an Atlanta disc jockey, about a new Elvis fan club in town and promptly joined thinking that it would help pass the time as my body healed. The Can't Get Enough of King Elvis Fan Club was run by Louise and Watson McCurley, a super couple devoted to Elvis. Some of the members bordered on the fanatical side, but on the whole it was a good group who gathered in Elvis' name to do charity work. Our goal was to promote Elvis's good name through good deeds. It was a great experience and I became life-long friends with several members - Beverly Mickle, Dorothy Campbell, Joyce Biddie Hulsey, and Sue McCasland. I became more involved with the club and was very close friends with the McCurleys for a time. With all that I was going through I enjoyed the diversion.

It was at a private showing of "Elvis on Tour," sponsored by the fan club in early November 1972, that I met Joyce Biddie Hulsey.

She had driven over from Birmingham for the movie and we became immediate friends. Joyce presented a striking appearance. Both of us are tall natural blondes, but that is the end of our similarities. Joyce speaks very softly, where I, on the other hand, do not have her understated demeanor. I am a little too exuberant and never seem to hold back when maybe I should. However, our personalities complimented one another and right off we felt we had known each other forever. When I met her she was wearing a white mink jacket with a blue fox collar and the next day I went to Rich's in search of a mink jacket; I thought that it might make me look more sophisticated. I settled on a darker one, but with the same blue fox collar; I always felt like a movie star when I wore it.

As a special treat fan club members, Janice Gwin, Angie Williams, and I planned a trip to Las Vegas in February 1973 to see Elvis at the Hilton. Nothing we had heard prepared us for what we saw when we arrived in Las Vegas. Every billboard screamed "ELVIS at The Hilton!" The hotel lobby was a circus. Metallic Elvis posters of all shapes and sizes adorned the walls and hung from crystal chandeliers; cardboard discs fashioned like records covered the hallways. Souvenirs were being sold everywhere - in typical Elvis style, the proceeds from the souvenirs were going to a charity; this time for deaf children. The glamour of the casino was anti-climatic in contrast to the Elvis hype and we preferred cruising the lobby and soaking up the atmosphere rather than seeing the famed strip. Never had we seen so much Elvis stuff and we loved it. Even the showroom menus bore his face.

We talked to everyone we could to find out any information about Elvis and the shows. We had been told that the more you tipped the Maitre d' the closer you got to the stage. We were very inexperienced in these matters, so on the afternoon of our arrival I went down to see the Maitre d', Emelio Muscelli. I wanted to know how much it would cost and blatantly offered him money. He quietly assured me that all his guests were treated equally and money was unnecessary. I left his office feeling that I had failed to secure a front row seat and sadly went back to the hotel room. As the time for the dinner show approached, we went down to the lobby and stood in line to be admitted to the showroom. Emilio's assistant, Bill, stood at the podium checking reservations and table locations. As he turned us over to a waiter to seat us, I noticed a gentlemen in the line to the left of us slip some money into Bill's hand... a beam of light suddenly cut through the fog in my brain, so I quickly asked Janice and Angie for some money as we were being escorted to our seats. The waiter started to seat us midway back in the showroom, until I pressed $20 into his hand. He smiled and bowed slightly then took us down to one of the tables, which extended from the stage at the far right. It wasn't the best seat in the house, but it was considerably closer than our original seat would have been... now that I knew the procedure, we'd get even better seats for the midnight show.

We ordered our dinner as we looked about at the other Elvis fans and took in the gaudy, glitzy splendor of the gilded showroom. After we had eaten, the opening acts began and finally Elvis appeared on the stage. He was wearing a white jumpsuit, glittering with jewels glitter that glinted off the spotlight. WOW! What quality did this man possess that his mere presence could send throngs of people into fits of hysteria? Every time I saw him in person it always seemed like a dream, because he had such an unearthly quality about him. I wished for another opportunity to meet with him, even if just for a brief moment to share my memories of him and let him know how much he had meant to me for all those years; I also wanted to thank him for sending me that letter when I was in the hospital and needed uplifting... I wanted a chance to relate to him in a relaxed atmosphere to sit and listen to what was on his mind and laugh with him about the way of things. I just bet that a person in his position could use a friend who didn't want anything more from him than to just be there for him; someone he didn't have to live up to his image around or worry about saying the wrong thing. I really wanted to be that friend for him, because I felt that he had been a friend to me so many times... even if he didn't know it. But he was a superstar with millions of fans clamoring to be near him and I had already been granted a precious moment that I was always grateful for... naturally I wanted more.

For all my passion over Elvis, I can't say that I felt a sexual attraction or fantasized about him. He just seemed like someone warm and loving that you would want to be close to, but my dream wasn't to be his lover. I guess I didn't want to be like every other woman he encountered; my goal was to be someone different in his life - a friend who asked nothing in return; just to be there for him if he needed a friend.

None of us were close enough to get a scarf, but that was ok for then. After the show we had a little time to kill, so we went back to the room and planned our strategy for the midnight performance. We knew we had to have more money to get better seats, so we dug a little deeper into our shallow pockets. We went back down a little early and got in line for the midnight show. When we reached the podium I placed the folded $30 quietly into Bill's hand. We were then escorted to the first row of booths by the stage, behind the tables, right in the center. It was much better seating because we were right at the base of the ramp that extended from the stage. Elvis had walked down that ramp earlier and if we left our seats and walked just a couple of feet, one of us might actually get a scarf. However once the show started we were too mesmerized to move. He was so close you could see the sweat running down his face, the shine on his white boots, and the twinkle in his eyes. As we soaked up the music and the man, we also learned a little more about how things worked at an Elvis concert. Girls in the audience were giving Elvis gifts - all kinds of things, like humorous statues, Budweiser hats, artistic likenesses of himself, and roses; anything to get his attention and garner a much - desired scarf and more desired kiss. Another gimmick that I would learn to use to my advantage.

We saw two more shows the following night and due to our limited funds our seating didn't get any better. But this trip was a great preparation for future trips. We rode the elevator up to the penthouse where Elvis stayed only to be turned away by security guards. Hey, it was worth a try! We went to Colonel. Parker's office and met his assistant Tom Diskin. The next morning, before we left, we actually met and talked to the Colonel himself. Looking back, it was a rather uneventful trip, but at the time it was great

and we enjoyed every minute of it. When we got home we learned Elvis had gotten the flu and had done only one show per night for the remaining two weeks and on one night he cancelled - a very rare occurrence.

The "Aloha From Hawaii" television special was broadcast via satellite to over 40 countries on January 14, 1973, but in America we had to wait until April 4th to watch it. By then cuts from the concert were playing on the radio and we had heard the album, but seeing was, believing. What a moment it was as he walked onto a world stage with his name flashing in dozens of languages on a fifty-foot high screen behind him - only he was larger than life enough to fill that stage. Has there ever been a more iconic moment in Pop Culture? Never before had the world press been so united in expressing their adoration for an entertainer. This was the apex of his career; on stage and behind the scenes, his entire array of talents and generosity were on display.

In 1961 Elvis had performed a benefit concert in Hawaii to raise the funds that completed the Arizona War Memorial in Pearl

Harbor, because congress didn't see fit to appropriate the needed stipend after 20 years of trying. On this evening the Kui Lee Cancer Fund would be the recipient of the proceeds. Lee was a Hawaiian singer/songwriter known for his balladic masterpiece, "I'll Remember You," and had died of cancer prematurely at the age of 34. Elvis not only performed the show for charity, he also bought the first ticket, making a donation of $1,500. Actor Jack Lord, star of "Hawaii 5-0," paid $1000 for his ticket. Only days before the show, Elvis had shown up at his condominium out of the blue and presented Lord with the belt to his costume - they were stitching jewels into a new belt right till the last minute before Elvis walked on. The event raised $75,000 in total - $50,000 more than expected - but more importantly the concert raised awareness and focused a spotlight on the cause, which brought in other donations.

I sat cross-legged on the floor about two feet from the television to be sure I could hear and see everything. I loved the exciting camera angles and the production pieces showing the islands as Elvis sang Hawaiian songs from his repertoire. (This segment was recorded after the concert and seen only by American audiences; you'll notice he doesn't have his belt anymore.) The background singers were all in their island whites and looked so heavenly. Elvis looked terrific and sounded incredible; his choice of music was mature and highlighted his amazing evolution as a vocalist. His movements were subdued, but his stance was omnipotent. I later learned that he had a pulled muscle in his leg and was in terrible pain for this concert. With his great ability as a showman he was able to make it work to his advantage, because his lack of gyrations gave him a regal bearing. The audience was very responsive and it showcased how special his loving relationship was with his adoring fans. They gave him leis, and crosses, and island trinkets, as he sent scarves floating into a sea of outstretched hands and knelt to share tender touches and sweet kisses with them.

I practically memorized every look and gesture he made in that concert - the way his eyes set the mood for a sincere ballad, the way he pounded the microphone against his chest during, "Love Me," the way he strolled and strutted along the runway, and undulated across it during, "Fever," the way he cracked up when he threw the glass of water at Charlie Hodge at the beginning of, "Big Hunk of Love," the way he acted like that little girl was pulling him off the stage, and, maybe most of all, how he stood poised during the flute solo of "The American Trilogy."... the vision of him exhaling and blowing the front of his hair up off of his forehead, while gearing up for the explosive finale of that song the way only he could perform it, still enthralls me every time I see it.

At the end of his next to last song, he walked to the edge of the runway then casually unhooked his opulent belt and, with a sly smile on his face, tossed it into the crowd. I was stunned sitting at home seeing him do it, but the audience went wild. While he dedicated his beloved closing number especially to the people of Hawaii, Charlie fastened his "American Eagle" cape loosely about his shoulders. As he hit the last note, his body contorted awkwardly then stooped, his neck twisted slightly and twitched as he reached behind his head. Then in one fluid motion he grace-fully pulled his bejeweled cape off and slung it into the audience, as he dropped to one knee with both arms extended, grinning from ear to ear, while the band and the singers held the crescendo to exalt him in his moment of triumph. He was enjoying the pan-demonium he had created and lingered to savor this time and place in his history. He rose and began a quick victory lap across the front of the stage. He pointed and winked to acknowledge his group and the staff of the show then struck several poses for the audience. Someone handed him a crown, which he gratefully accepted, but refused to put on his head. He may have been the king of the entertainment world, but he was a down to earth Christian in his heart and soul. He handled it perfectly, because the sight of him giving a farewell shakka wave into the camera, while holding the crown he deserved humbly at his side, is the image that most vividly captured the essence of the man.

PROMISED LAND

In March 1973, I was again hospitalized due to chronic phlebitis and in April I suffered the miscarriage of my daughter, whom I had named Emily Elizabeth. Later in April I was again hospitalized due to a massive hematoma pressing on my femoral nerve, which was cutting off circulation to my legs. The McCurley's paid me a visit and told me that Elvis would be in Atlanta at The Omni on June 21st, just a couple of months away. I got so excited that when the nurse came in to take my blood pressure she remarked that it was a little high! I just had to get well and get out of that hospital and be ready when Elvis came to town; I would need determination and prayers to work a miracle.

By the time June 21st had arrived I was back on my feet and ready to go. I had willed myself to be healthy enough to attend and was rewarded with the best news; Elvis had added four more shows - an evening show on June 29th, a matinee and evening show on June 30, and an evening show for July 3rd. There were five concerts in Atlanta in a two-week period and I had front row center seats for every show. I wanted to look my best, so before the first show I spent the day at the beauty shop getting my hair in an up-do and having my make-up done. All around the city there were billboards and placards announcing the coming of the King of Rock & Roll. It wasn't as saturated as Vegas, but the advertising was extensive.

The Omni was filled to capacity, as it would be for every show. Before the first show started, Louise and Watson McCurley were escorted backstage to meet Elvis where they were given a huge stuffed hound dog and an orange scarf, which she tied around her neck. I was so excited for them. The fact that they had just been so close to Elvis moments before added energy to our group and we were on the edge of our seats before the lights were lowered and the kettledrums announced the coming magic. The excitement arcing through the audience was electric. A hush fell as every person waited breathlessly... then there were shrieks and cries of, "THERE HE IS!" The Omni exploded with screams, applause, and thousands of popping flashbulbs as Elvis strode around the stage. Then he took his guitar from Charlie Hodge after a moment of banter that only they could hear and approached the microphone. He smiled and nodded then his head began popping along to get the into the groove of, "CC Rider," and he went rolling right along as he went into "I Got A Woman/Amen."

The songs went quickly and the show had a fast pace. Elvis took a moment to talk and joke with the audience in between songs then went about hitting notes to the rafters, while karate kicking and slashing his way through the songs. He became serious when he performed his Grammy Award Winning sacred classic, "How Great Thou Art," which brought him a standing ovation. He responded to the cheers by repeating the last verse, which brought more accolades from his admiring audience. He sang The Beatles hit, "Something," and dedicated it to his girlfriend, Linda Thompson. Vernon and Lisa Marie were also present at the shows and I could see them from where I was. My personal favorite number was, "The American Trilogy." Now, being a staunch Southerner at a concert in the Deep South, when "Dixie" was played, we always stood up - it is after all the Southern National Anthem, so many of us were standing from the first note. As he reached the crescendo of "Battle Hymn of the Republic" the spotlight shone on the American Flag unfurled above the stage and the entire audience roared their approval, applauding for minutes after the song ended - this happened at every show, but the first time that the audience spontaneously combusted like that remains my all time favorite memory.

I managed to get through the first show in somewhat of a daze, never screaming nor running for a scarf, just looking and watching and applauding until my hands were sore. Well, maybe I did yell a little. Finally it was ending and Elvis was on one knee directly in front of me, cape extended by both arms, head bowed to acknowledge the thunderous ovation. He looked directly into my eyes and winked. He then pulled at one end of the orange scarf around his neck, nodded at me then popped it toward me. I remained standing by my seat as several women scuffled for the scarf. James Caughley, who worked for Elvis, he reached over and plucked the scarf from one of the girls then brought it to me. "He wanted YOU to have this," he insisted, as he placed it in my hands. I was stunned as I clutched the warm, wet scarf. Could Elvis have somehow recognized me or was I just in his line of fire? Whatever the reason, I quickly placed the scarf in my purse and tried to fend off the curious and angry women who were willing to fight for it.

Elvis was also a seasoned raconteur that had great stories to tell about the legendary moments of his fabled career and he'd have the place doubled over with laughter. He knew how to completely entertain the crowd, so that both he and his audience were drained of every last drop of emotionalism before the adventure was over; in the end you felt like you had gone through it all with him... that was the nature of the symbiotic relationship he had with his audience. Before there had been an epic grandeur to his shows, they were choreographed productions that were dazzling and though Elvis always had interacted with his audiences, he remained across a divide. But as time wore on he relaxed and felt more at home with us more than ever before. It was almost as if he didn't have to put on a show for us, because we loved him for who he was, so he let down his guard and let us see him beyond the image, by being himself - a fun loving guy that enjoyed off the wall behavior, bizarre gadgets and epic music. In some ways, we were his eyes to the world, because the only time he was turned loose amongst society was while he was on stage, so he depended on us to keep him in the loop so that he wouldn't lose touch with humanity. Along with show business tales, he also discussed the situations in his life, the lawsuits, his illnesses, things that happened around the house the other day; we were like a group of friends catching up and keeping up with his life and times as much as his records and concerts and the audiences went away with a bigger piece of the man than they could have gotten from just the performance of a song.

After the show, some of my friends were taken to the hotel to meet Elvis, Toni Gilbert, Judy Profitt McDonald, Beverly Brown Davis, Linda Hicks Jackson, and Sherry McLaughlin Hague. Toni reported afterwards, "Like anyone who had the honor to meet him, it was love at first sight." I knew this to be true from my own precious encounter. They were so impressed that the next day they went to the fine jewelry department and bought a magnificent piece of jewelry, without their husbands knowing. "How do you tell your husband you're buying a piece of jewelry for a millionaire?" quipped Toni. It was a cross that had seven tourmaline stones down and five across with a diamond in the center. When Elvis came back to town a couple of weeks later they planned to give it to him.

For the next three shows I was in the same area in the audience. Elvis seemed to acknowledge me with a wave, a wink or a smile at different times. At the matinee I sat near a woman who had dressed her son in a white jumpsuit and cape. He looked to be about three years old. At the end of the show Elvis gave the boy his belt and cape! After the third show Elvis threw me a blue scarf, but it was grabbed out of my hands by Sandra Sommers, a fan club member. She felt justified her rude behavior by proclaiming loudly that I already had one. I let her keep it without making a scene to retrieve what was rightfully mine; I refused to behave in any manner less than a lady. But I couldn't help noticing the frown on some of the faces of the security guys towards her. When the final show was ending, Elvis nodded directly to me - no doubt about it this time - and held out a white scarf. I rose from my chair and approached the stage on legs that were fittingly shaky. I knew that I was going to be touched again by ELVIS! ELVIS! ELVIS! He gently placed the scarf around my neck and gave me a peck on the cheek as I melted. I thanked him so much and returned to my seat unable to believe that I had been given two scarves, one letter, a hug and now a nuzzle from him in one lifetime. It felt incredible! The first thing I did was wipe his sweat off my cheek and hair with the damp scarf... though not all of it. There was a lot of jealousy from some of the other fan club members, which I could not understand. I wished that they could all have been given scarves and an intimate exchange with Elvis, but it certainly wasn't in my control and you can bet I wasn't giving any of them my scarves.

After the show, we all went to Stouffers, where Elvis was staying. Somehow we managed to beat the limo there and just as we were walking up to the sidewalk Elvis drove right by us. I was so startled that I tripped, I stumbled, I fell... completely embarrassed I picked myself up and went into the lobby. Toni, Linda, Judy, Sherry, and Beverly told Charlie Hodge that they wanted to present a very special gift to Elvis. He said that it was so crowded that only three of them could go up. Toni, Linda, and Beverly followed Charlie up to Elvis' suite. In the meantime one of Elvis' bodyguards, Dick Grob, came up and asked if I was the one who had gone head over heals onto the sidewalk. Sheepishly I nodded and he revealed that Elvis had cracked up when he saw me, but hoped that I hadn't hurt myself. I smiled to think that I had given Elvis a good laugh and thought that it was so considerate for him to ask after me. While attending his concerts, I could tell that he was very aware of what went on around him. He really cared that people might get hurt or wronged in the vortex of excitement that surrounded him, so he paid attention out of concern.

When the girls got upstairs, Charlie reminded Elvis that he had met them when he was in town the previous week. After taking the time to get their names he thanked them kindly for coming to his shows. When they gave him the gift and the card Elvis was truly touched that they had gone out of their way to give him something so beautiful; I think that he was surprised by the largesse of such a gift... this was something like Elvis would give out to the fans and not something he would expect in return. Elvis opened the card and after reading the sentiment he recited the names signed on the inside. When he got to Toni's name he sang, "Toni O'Darlin," which is close to "Tarnell Darling" from "Lawdy Miss Clawdy." Toni then told him that the other girls who had helped pay for the cross were down in the lobby, so Elvis sent Kenny Hicks, of the Stamps, down to get all of them. Elvis then gave the card to Linda Thompson and told her to save it for him. Once everyone was gathered, Linda put the cross around his neck. Looking at it, Elvis admired, "This is fantastic! I needed a new cross; I gave my last one to Don Rickles."

After that they settled in and got comfortable. He asked the girls how the sound was in The Omni and which songs that they liked the best. They all agreed that they liked all the songs that he did, but Toni asked him to pretty please sing her favorite, "Help Me Make It Through the Night" and told him where they would be sitting. Sure enough, the next night when he came on stage, Elvis was wearing the cross and while fingering it he remarked, "It's great to be back in Atlanta with my good friends." Then he pointed to where they were seated and sang their request. The girls started screaming, crying, and hitting each other, knowing that he was singing it specially for them!

As for the now fabled cross, he only wore it several times before he gave it away. He almost lost it once in Las Vegas when the chain broke. A girl that was getting a scarf from him grabbed it right off of his neck and put it into her purse. Beverly was right there and went to Sonny West, so he could stop her from getting away with it. Later on the tour, a young girl kept trying to get a scarf and couldn't, because the bigger ladies were knocking her aside. Elvis saw her out there crying and stopped the show. To everyone's amazement he brought her onto the stage and put the cross around her neck. He then asked security to stay nearby, so that she didn't lose her necklace. That was Elvis and it was expected, so they didn't feel bad that he had given away their gift. Like he said, he'd given his last cross away too... and no doubt all the ones before that. It was given to him to do with as he saw fit and he chose to bestow it upon another. Gifts were like magic to Elvis. Once you used it the magic was gone until you gave it to someone else. If you bought him something nice or made him something special he would be so happy to receive it, because it meant you were thinking of him. He would show it around and really enjoy it for what it was then he would pass it along to someone that was overjoyed to receive it from him. For Elvis, giving and receiving was his way of bonding with you. It didn't matter if it was expensive jewelry and luxury cars when he was a superstar, or his bike and toys as a poor boy, Elvis was forever giving away the things he prized so that someone else could prize them too.

Giving the weeping little girl an expensive cross is a moment that is part of his legacy, but was retold and portrayed in so many different ways that for years, people disbelieved that it ever really happened; it was seen as an apocryphal tale, like George Washington and the cherry tree; Newton and the apple; Babe Ruth and the "Called Shot." For some reason in the 1979 T.V movie "Elvis," starring Kurt Russell, they depict Elvis in his gold lame` suit giving this necklace to the little girl at the concert he did in Hawaii after he got out of the Army. Other books have placed the event in different times and some have stated that the necklace was really some plastic concoction made by fans. The story of the cross was resurrected in 1988 on the program, "A Current Affair," when it was put up for auction. The family had held onto this treasure for many years, because of the sentimental value. They had managed to get along, but when financial ruin struck they had to let go of their most cherished possession. Even though it was worth a fortune to them it still broke their hearts to lose their family heirloom. I believe that Elvis would have been touched that they held onto it with love for so long, and pleased that they raised nearly a million dollars for this valuable artifact... Elvis changed their lives not once, but twice and it all began with a small group of hardworking, loving fans that wanted to show how deeply they cared for this great man.

This was Elvis; a man who didn't take a legitimate tax right off for his charitable donations, because he thought it ruined the whole spirit of giving. When Elvis was asked why he passed out dazzling jewels to his audience, he replied, "I can just feel out there that someone really needs it and that's my way of helping." ... oh how he touched lives!

FROM ELVIS PRESELY BOULEVARD

Later on during that summer of 1973 I went to Memphis via Tupelo with my mother to visit family. We went by Elvis' birthplace and took in the sights, as we walked along the streets of his life. When you see his humble beginnings, in a shack smaller than Lincoln's log cabin, you can't help but wonder what it must have been like for the family huddled in there together against the world and the elements. How did Elvis manage to become a dreamer under such difficult circumstances? We left Tupelo and headed for Memphis along Old Highway 78 as the Presleys had in 1948. (Later it was designated Elvis Presley Highway.) Crossing the state line into Memphis, I felt like I was home in my heart; my life has taken me many places, but I have always carried a part of Memphis with me wherever I go. As soon I was over the border, I headed straight for Graceland. Elvis was out on the road, but we talked to Uncle Vester.

He was just the nicest man and we chatted like old friends. The great thing about him was that he had heard a thousand Elvis stories over the years and he loved every one of them. He also had a thousand Elvis stories of his own and over the years he shared them with fans. Elvis would kid around and say, "Heaven has Saint Peter and Graceland has my Uncle Vester." A perfect tribute to a wonderful man. I was in the bosom of Elvis world and I felt serene.

My health was slowly on the mend and I was busy with my 12-year-old son, George Randall, as well as a failing marriage. The accident and the loss of our child had driven a wedge between us that seemed to only grow wider. As Christmas approached Janice Gwin and Yvonne Stallings invited me to go with them to Memphis for the weekend and I couldn't wait. It was December 15 and Elvis was always at Graceland for Christmas. They wanted to go hang out at the gatehouse in the hopes of seeing him. I brought my son with me, and Joyce met up with us in Memphis. I immediately took my son to my aunt's house for the night. It was snowing and I wasn't sure what the evening would bring and I didn't want him to get cold if we were outside for very long.

We brought gifts with us and gave them to Harold Loyd, whom everyone called, "Cousin Harold." His mother, Rhetha, was Gladys' sister. Rhetha died when Harold was a boy, so he went back and forth among the kin and practically grew up with Elvis. Typical of the family, he was so kindly and considerate as he thanked us very much on Elvis' behalf. I brought a hat for Lisa Marie that was crocheted by my friend, Louise Bettis, which had blonde Shirley Temple curls hanging down the back, and I gave Elvis silk, black pillowcases with ELVIS embroidered in pink letters on it. Joyce had crocheted a cape for Lisa Marie, so that she could be like her daddy. "Cousin" Harold then took us aside and confided that Elvis was in the recording studio that night. Janice and Yvonne didn't want to go to and decided to wait around at the gates for a while. Since Stax Recording Studio wasn't that far from Graceland, Joyce and I headed over there. It was located in the old Capitol Theater building and named for its founders, Jim Stewart and his sister Estelle Axton. Elvis had been recording at American

Sound Studios since 1969, but his friend Marty Lacker worked for Stax and he got Elvis to schedule some studio time there.

Elvis was recording songs that were later released on the albums Good Times and Promised Land. Joyce and I confidently walked to the doors, but they were locked. There was a security guard, but we didn't know him, so we didn't bother him. We just went back to Joyce's car and sat down hoping that someone we knew would come out so maybe we could get in. You could hear music playing from the sound truck in the lot and we listened, while we shivered and watched the snowfall. In about an hour, we saw the security guard approaching our car with two cups in his hand. He stopped on the passenger side of the car and I lowered the window. "The man inside thought you might be cold," he intoned. He handed us two cups of hot chocolate and walked away. We looked at each other questioningly, shrugged and drank the deliciously warm chocolate. "The Man?"

A few minutes later, he came back out and walked purposefully toward our car. This time I thought he was for sure going to run us off for loitering. He'd been patient, even kind, but we were

48

pushing it. I rolled down the window and got ready to comply with his request to leave... I never dreamed that he'd be asking us if we wanted to come into the studio and listen to the session. Before he had to ask us twice we were out of the car and on our way inside paradise. We were told that there could be no photographs, no questions, and no interruptions; once we willingly and happily agreed, we were let in. Elvis made no gesture of acknowledgement toward us, but if he knew what was going on all around him in a sold out madhouse, he was certainly aware of the goings on inside the studio.

He was very professional and very much a perfectionist in what he was doing, repeating certain parts, changing tempos, sometimes laughing and clowning and sometimes fussing. My favorite song of the session was, "Loving Arms." They still had a few songs to record and we had a ringside seat, so we settled in. He looked terrific in a burgundy corduroy shirt with a short cape attached, black pants and black boots. Most other entertainers didn't dress as sharp on stage as he did in the studio. He and Kathy Westmoreland seemed to be very much attuned to one another and I don't mean just musically. We wondered if there was something kindling between them. They just would catch each other's eye when a particular lyric was sung or give each other a meaningful look - they had tremendous chemistry.

At about 3 am. we were asked to leave, as Sonny went out and warmed up Elvis' car - the white Stutz with the mink seats! We decided not to wait for him to come out, and went on back to Howard Johnson's on Elvis Presley Boulevard (now The Graceland Inn) where we were staying. Well, imagine our surprise when about an hour later we saw Elvis escorting Kathy to her room only a few doors down from ours! Naturally once again we didn't bring our cameras. So, getting up our nerve, we just, as polite as we could, walked out into the hall and casually said, "Hello," to him. Elvis looked over at us with a big smile and replied by asking, "Don't you girls ever sleep?" We all laughed together then he was curious to know if we liked what we heard that night. See he did know that we were there! We were puzzled as to why we had been invited in, but we didn't want to mess up this golden opportunity, so instead we got some pictures out for him to pretty please sign. Naturally the pen wouldn't write when he got to my name; he mumbled something about needing another pen and being tired, which made me feel guilty for bothering him for an autograph. I have wished a thousand times that I had bugged him for a picture instead! Joyce and I never wanted to impose on the fragile relationship we had with Elvis, whatever it was, and tried to act nonchalant, thereby never bringing our cameras or making pests of ourselves. We knew that flashbulbs irritated his eyes and we didn't want to contribute to that either. In addition we had heard that he requested his employees not take any pictures, so we just wanted to honor his wishes. We swore to keep the secret of his whereabouts and he thanked us then sent us to bed.

The very next night our friend Colleen Taylor, from Las Vegas, came into town and went to the Memphian Theater where she met Elvis outside and managed to get a picture taken with him... that lucky lady! ... and don't they just look great together!

George Randall was growing into a big fan and it was a great shared experience for us. He couldn't go off on my little excursions, because he played football and soccer and didn't want to miss the games, so we'd fill each other in on the details of our adventures when I'd get back. I was glad to have him with me on this special Christmas trip. It was nearly daylight when I went to pick him up at my aunt's. He wanted to go to Graceland, so we took him to the gatehouse. We had to go back to the motel to get our belongings, but my son wanted to stay there, so at Harold's insistence we left him there. When we came back to get him he was full of excitement, because Harold had opened the gates for Elvis and Elvis had smiled and waved right at him. I sure wish that I had been there, but at the same time I was glad that he had an Elvis story that was all his own - just like I had when I was his age.

I first learned of the March 1974 tour from Joyce. She had secured good seats for the March 6, show in Montgomery, Alabama, having been first in line when they went on sale. I started planning to give Elvis something special on stage and decided on a lei of pink miniature carnations, which I strung by hand - completed it contained sixty-three flowers. It was in Montgomery that I first met Sue McCasland who would later start the Elvis Now Fan Club of San Jose, California. Sue and I were not immediate friends, something we look back on and laugh about now. She was a schoolteacher who went onto become the Principal of a middle school. She was very proper and for some reason I felt intimidated by her. However, as I got to know her, I learned she was warm and trusting and we've become great friends. She was privy to a special friendship with Elvis and I was relatively new to the Elvis scene, so I didn't understand a lot of the conversation about some of the entourage. I listened intently as Sue and Joyce discussed strategies of how to get close to Elvis during the show, but my excitement was too great to remain quiet for very long and I asked a lot of questions.

Joyce had front row center seats for her and Sue, however my seat was on the front row, but over to the side. Since I had already made the lei, I gave it to a little girl named Robin - the daughter of Joyce's former employer - to give to Elvis. As the warm-up acts started, I was sorry to hear Jackie Kahane had not changed his jokes a bit. I noticed Colonel Parker sitting up front with the police officers assigned to security. The Sweet Inspirations put on a great show and then came the interminable intermission. Finally "2001: A Space Odyssey" began and WOW! There was Elvis, dressed in a white jumpsuit with red and blue beaded firebirds, without the cape. That old twinkle was in his blue eyes and we knew that we were in for a great show.

As Elvis opened with "CC Rider" the audience began to scream their heads off and he chided, "Hey y'all, wait a minute; I ain't done nothing yet!" Elvis acknowledged Joyce and Robin right away; Robin bore a striking resemblance to Lisa Marie and Elvis seemed to be singing right to her. After "I Got a Woman/Amen" Elvis addressed the audience, "Good evening ladies and gentlemen, my name is Glenn Campbell... we hope you enjoy our show this afternoon; we're going to do everything we can to make you happy. These flashbulbs, man. They're going choom-choom-choom." Then he turned to the people seated behind the band and asked, "What are y'all doing hanging from the ceiling up there?"

He started to sing, "Love Me," and about halfway through the first verse he took off his first navy blue scarf, pointed to Robin and handed the scarf to Colonel Parker, who gave it to her. She was so thrilled! Joyce asked the Colonel if Robin could give Elvis the lei and he gave his permission. Elvis then sang, "Trying to Get to You," and his voice was super. Next was "All Shook Up," then "Teddy Bear," and "Don't' Be Cruel." As the introduction to "Love Me Tender" was played, he remarked, "It's basically very hot up here!" Then he walked over to the stage where Joyce was holding Robin with the lei and said, "Come here, baby." The stage was especially low and Joyce raised Robin right up there so that he could kiss her on the cheek then he put another scarf around her neck; she hugged him in return and placed my lei around his neck... the crowd was touched by the endearing moment. He wore the lei for the remainder of the song and Charlie placed it on the piano when Elvis took it off. Joyce passed the second scarf to me, as I had made the lei. After a rousing rendition of, "Polk Salad Annie" Elvis pleaded, "Let me get my breath back," and walked over in front of Joyce and inquired, "What do you want honey, my pants, my belt, another scarf?" Oh how I wished that he'd made me an offer like that!

He then requested that The Stamps sing, "Why Me Lord," which was followed by the introduction of the band, with special attention being paid to Charlie, who is from Decatur, Alabama. Governor George Wallace had come back from a meeting in Washington, D.C. early, just to see Elvis, and was seated near the stage. Elvis thanked Governor Wallace for making it "Elvis Presley Week" in Alabama and stated that he also had been made an Honorary Colonel of the State. Then he prodded, "You know what I can't do?" Glen D. started the intro to "I Can't Stop Loving You," and Elvis called out, "Wait a minute!" as he finished his water. "You know," he chuckled, "I could sing me about 200 songs to that intro!" Finally he began the song and followed it with, "Trilogy" which received the usual well-deserved standing ovation. "Let Me Be There" was so well received that he sang the chorus twice.

Elvis signaled for the house lights to be turned up, and when they were he picked up the lei and placed it around Charlie's neck. Charlie then put it back around Elvis' neck. Elvis grabbed Colonel Parker's white cap and paraded around the stage in cap and flowers, just having a grand old time - he was simply adorable. By then, I had seen a dozen performances and this show far surpassed any of the others, including Atlanta. He was in fantastic shape, his voice was beautiful and far-reaching, and he was in a wonderful mood. Elvis did a one-of-a-kind version of, "Funny How Time Slips Away," that will forever be remembered by all who heard it. He grabbed the mike stand and said, "I'd like to thank the Academy... " and as he sat it down it broke. He turned to Kathy and clowned, "Look at me Kathy!" And they both cracked up. He introduced Colonel Parker as, "The gentleman whose hat I stole." Vernon received a warm reception when he was introduced and Elvis teased, "That's enough Daddy. You've got to watch him, man, he's dangerous!" As he started to say, "It's been fun" or "It's been a fun evening," he got his tongue twisted around and said, "It's really been a fun..." He paused, looked at Charlie and asked, "Been a FUN?" He chuckled as he thanked us all and brought it home with, "Can't Help Falling In Love." He exited the stage wearing the lei and leaving in his wake some very happy people wanting more... as we left we were already looking forward to his upcoming shows in Knoxville and Memphis.

"GOT MY MOJO WORKING"

I was thoroughly bitten by the Elvis bug now. My marriage had totally fallen apart and Elvis provided an escape from reality - a nostalgic look back, a fountain of youth, a well of hope springing eternal. It wasn't divinity that was guiding me to be there, it was my own freewill, but it was a calling. I knew that being immersed in this culture would be the most epic aspect of my simple life and I wanted to enrich myself by basking in these moments every time I possibly could; I didn't know where the path would lead, but I was dedicated to following it to the end. Every show, every touch, each look, another scarf, was life affirming and strengthened my connection to him, which made me feel very special; I knew there was a reason for being there even if it wasn't apparent to me.

Joyce was planning a trip to Memphis for the concerts on March 16th and 17th. I already had plans to go with my friend and hairdresser, Norma Brancale. We were going to stay at the Howard Johnson's, so we agreed to meet. It was around this time that Joyce told me how she made extra money while on the circuit. She took concert pictures and sold them in sets of ten - she never overcharged and her pictures were good quality. So I purchased a used Yashika 35 mm camera, got a few tips on angles and lighting from Joyce, and from Judy Palmer of Seattle, Washington, and awaited my first opportunity to take a photo of him.

Norma and I flew into Memphis and rented a car. The city was in an ecstatic state and Elvis Presley Boulevard was bumper to bumper. Fans were lined up at Graceland by the gate and all along the street. What's interesting to note is that, although Elvis had been back touring for some five years by then, he had not performed a concert in Memphis since 1961. We knew most of Elvis' entourage stayed at the Howard Johnson's, so that's where we got rooms. We were not surprised to see Kathy, as well as James Burton, and Charlie Hodge milling about. We quickly located

Joyce and her friend, Shannon, then we all went to lunch to discuss logistics for the concert, before returning to the hotel to get ready. Everyone kept their doors open and wandered from room to room; the place was wall-to-wall with Elvis fans, and even some of Elvis' staff were among those making the rounds - they were treated like celebrities too.

The crowd began to thin out as people left for the Mid-South Coliseum and a bus arrived to pick up band members; we were sort of straggling behind, because we were taking it all in. Norma and Shannon had elected to go onto the concert, while Joyce and I stayed behind. Suddenly there were several Memphis policemen on our floor and two black limousines pulled up in the back. Excitedly, we deduced that Elvis was there and not at Graceland after all! We stayed in our room, but left our door open as we walked back and forth to the balcony to check on the limos below. We were standing out there when a Memphis policeman, whose name was Summers, stuck his head in our door. He thanked us for not telling anyone that we knew that Elvis was there. We just smiled and assured them that we weren't the type to tell secrets. In a moment, Joe Esposito and Dick Grob came to our room and asked us if we needed tickets. I guess they thought that if we had tickets we would have already been gone, because time was growing short - Elvis always timed his arrivals, so he could walk into the building and hit the stage without breaking stride. We told them we had tickets and they said that if ever in the future we needed tickets to just see them and it would all be taken care of. This was great, but puzzling as we had never had any previous contact with Joe, and my only encounter with Dick had been the time I tripped on the curb in Atlanta, which I was sure he didn't remember. They weren't flirting; they were just being so nice. We thanked them and told them that we appreciated the offer, but we usually bought tickets from someone who had connections with the arena where Elvis appeared, so that we could have front row seats. Joe reiterated that if the time ever came that we ever needed tickets, all we had to do was ask! We chitchatted for a few minutes then they had to get going. Joe asked if were ready to leave, but we said that we would need another minute - we wanted to wait and see Elvis walkout even if we were late getting to the show.

We stood in our doorway and in moments, there he was. Not only was Elvis in the hotel, he was in the room right next to ours! He walked right past us, and we were mesmerized. He was wearing a black leather coat with a blue fox collar - the identical collar to the ones on mine, and Joyce's jackets! I'm sure he had to notice that we had on the same blue fox collar; they were so unique that they stood out. He smiled at us and we beamed at him as he turned to the right to go down the steps. We never considered asking for an autograph since we knew that he was in a hurry; we were just happy to see him up close and in person again. We raced to the balcony with cameras in hand to catch him getting

into the limo. I was so excited to take my very first picture of Elvis. I had him lined up, but I must have hesitated, because by the time I took the shot, I was a split second off and only got his body. Just as he was ducking his head to get in he stopped, looked up at us perched above and wanted to know, "Are you girls going to the show?" We answered in tandem, "Yes." He directed, "Well c'mon,

you'd better hurry." That was close enough to an invitation, so we bounded down the stairs, jumped into Joyce's Thunderbird and fell right in behind Elvis. There we were racing through the streets of Memphis, following the limousine of Elvis Presley and being escorted by the Memphis police! What a hoot! At one point Elvis turned around, waved at us then broke up laughing; we were waving at him and going nuts - it was sheer euphoria. I tried to take another picture and got the back of his head in the limo. As we turned into the coliseum parking lot, the police thought that we were part of the motorcade and waved us in. We parked the car and headed for the entrance as the limo went into the underground of the building.

We reached our seats by the stage just as Elvis was walking on. We both still had on our coats and we were rather conspicuous in the spotlight. Elvis looked down at us and teased, "Hey, haven't I seen you girls somewhere before?" We grinned like idiots and nodded in unison. It seemed that from then on he singled us out for extra special attention. He brought us up individually for a scarf, so that we did not have to grapple for it or rush the stage; he placed it around our necks and gave us kisses - on the lips! We couldn't believe our good fortune. Just as the show was coming to a close, we left our seats in order to be in our car to follow him back to the motel. However, one limo went back to Howard Johnson's and the other one, with Elvis in it, went a different direction. We were puzzled, but had no choice except to return to the motel. We met up with some friends who had seen the exchanges between us and Elvis at the concert and they were full of questions about how we had gotten to know him... naturally we couldn't answer and that made them all the more curious.

We went by Graceland and "Cousin" Harold told us that Elvis had moved over to the Rivermont, which was a Holiday Inn. We decided to grab a bite to eat before the evening show and naturally went over there. At the restaurant Charlie Hodge saw us and came right over to our table and joined us. He told us confidentially that B. J. Thomas had been dressed in a white jumpsuit and ensconced in Graceland to throw off the fans. They had even sent a limo to pick him up and drive him around Memphis. Then he imparted, "Hey, Elvis really appreciated y'all not telling anyone where he was." We smiled at the idea of Elvis Presley making a comment about us. By the time we found out there was no one to tell, but even if we had known we would have kept his secret gladly - anything for Elvis! We could have called the press and the world the night that we saw him with Kathy, so we had earned the praise. Charlie asked us if we were moving over to the Rivermont where they would all be staying that night. We told him that we were remaining at that Howard Johnson's and we had just come over to the Rivermont to eat dinner.

We were joined by, Sonny, Red, and Dick. We all introduced ourselves to each other and when I said my name, Sonny probed, "Does anyone call you Sandi?" Even though I replied in the negative, he decided, "Well you look like a Sandi to me and that's what I'm going to call you." From then on I was "Sandi." We talked about the show and the tour and shared some small talk. I told Red about seeing him in Macon a couple of years prior and about being originally from Memphis and visiting at Audubon Drive and we all talked like we were old friends. I could hardly finish my dinner for the butterflies in my stomach, but I was even more nervous after supper when they invited us upstairs - we weren't sure what to expect. Although we were both in unhappy marriages, we were not the promiscuous type, even for Elvis Presley, or his associates, so we were apprehensive about accepting their kind offer. It was not that we didn't find Dick, Sonny, and Red attractive - on the contrary. I thought Sonny West was a most ruggedly, handsome man and I admired his sternness with the fanatical fans - you felt safe with him around. I liked his soft-spoken demeanor, which was a contrast to his rough appearance. Then there was Red; what wasn't to like about him? He had charisma, personality, charm, and was also handsome - people didn't know that beneath his steel wool persona there was a soul of a poet. Dick was like "The boy next door," cute, fun, friendly, kind, and personable - tall, dark and handsome. They all presented this fierce exterior - that was their job - but were truly gentlemen. Their unusually respectful manners towards us were appreciated.

After the evening show we went back to the hotel. We saw Vernon who immediately came over to me, took my hand and declared that he never forgot a face - he was certain that he knew me from somewhere. Once again I told my story and he smiled and said that it was good to see me after so many years! I don't think he remembered me specifically - although he had sure seen me around - but he was polite and courteous. Then Elvis emerged from his room with Linda Thompson. She wore sandals and I could see that she had tiny flowers painted on her toenails - I thought that this was a very elegant touch. Elvis was wearing his karate ghee and looked so tired. "Honey," he cooed to me, "I know we've met before, but you'll have to excuse me, because I don't remember. I'm tired right now, but I know I have seen you at the shows." I stammered something about having met him many years ago and then shut up, because he really did look exhausted. Joyce and I thanked him for allowing us this time to visit with him; he smiled as he signed pictures for both of us then he and Linda went to bed.

Vernon invited us to sit down, as several other people began to filter into the room. It began to look like a more intimate evening than we were ready for and when it was obvious that Elvis and

Linda would not be coming back, we said our good-byes. We went back to our hotel room and congratulated ourselves for making it all the way inside of Elvis' inner sanctum and for holding our own in a set of sophisticated circumstances.

As we got to know the guys better over the years they never talked down to us, never used foul language in our presence, and always made us feel comfortable. Sonny and Red talked freely about their families and I think that made us better friends - there's nothing more beautiful than a man who openly loves his family. We had a flirtatious attraction that we enjoyed that never got out of hand. In their position they didn't need to "come on" to women and they didn't objectify women as sex objects. They appreciated our sincere intentions. After our encounter at the hotel with Elvis, we showed that we could be trusted and so we were accepted on that basis.

The Memphis shows were some of the best ever. If you don't believe me listen to the album Recorded Live In Memphis. (The album with Graceland on the cover.) He unveiled the "Memphis Medley" in that show and it was exhilarating. At one of the concerts Elvis remarked, "I have about 400 of my cousins here." Maybe that was why he was so inspired! The next afternoon was a replay of the day before. We were offered tickets to that show as well as the upcoming show in St. Louis and the closing show in Memphis, but I had to return home, much to my dismay, or I would have accepted those tickets. I've always regretted my decision to return home. Even though I knew there would be other times, each trip was momentous in its own right and who knows what wonders I missed - you can make new memories, but you can't make up for what never was... like a leaf floating in the stream; once it floats past, it is gone.

MR. SONGMAN

Elvis seemed to be playing in many nearby towns and I just couldn't pass up any opportunity to see him. I guess our faces became as familiar to the entourage as theirs were to us. Often Joyce and I would be joined by one or more of the group for lunch or dinner or just coffee and cokes. We enjoyed idle chat as well as light conversation about Elvis - we did not want to appear overeager or fanatical. We seemed to have been accepted as friends more than fans. We didn't consider ourselves "groupies," because the women who chased after the men in the entourage wanted only one thing - to get to Elvis by any means necessary. We had already met Elvis and had a building relationship with him, his family, and his closest entourrage. I believe it was a relief to them to be able to relax with us, knowing that we weren't trying to use them.

We saw Elvis change girlfriends from Linda Thompson to Sheila Ryan, and in-between there were constant one-night stands. Then Linda was back, in August 1974, when Joyce, Sue and I met in Las Vegas for the Elvis Summer Festival. We had been planning the trip for months, so you can imagine our disappointment when we walked into the Hilton on August 26 and were told that Elvis would not perform due to a bout with the flu! Later in the day a sign was placed at the Hilton entrance with the bleak announcement on it. Joyce had brought a beautiful lei for Elvis from Birmingham and we just hoped that he would perform on Tuesday, so it would last long enough for us to give it to him.

Monday night we went out of the Hilton, something unheard of for Elvis fans, and attended Johnny Tillotson's show in a lounge nearby. Johnny was from Jacksonville and used to date an acquaintance of mine, Ann Wester. In the audience was John Davidson, who proved to be not nearly the nice guy he appeared to be on television. We weren't really enjoying ourselves, so we returned to the hotel, which was strangely empty of any Elvis people. The next day we went down to see Emilio and he said that either Elvis or Bill Cosby would perform - there would be a show; he just wasn't sure which one would perform. The good news came later in the afternoon, when Dick told us that Elvis would go on. We attended four shows and were seated right next to the stage for every performance. Evidently our newfound friends had whispered something into Bill or Emilio's ear, for our money was no longer necessary to get those coveted seats. Also, we now stood in the "Invited Guest" line.

This was the period when Elvis began wearing two-piece leather and suede Victorian suits made by North Beach Leather, rather than his customary spangled jumpsuits. One suit was off-white leather with pastel flowers painted on the shoulders and down the legs of the pants. This outfit was a gift from one of his cousins. Another suit was buff colored suede with lots of sparkle and glitter on the back, shoulders and pants. Another was white leather with red stitching, which was still at the shop when we paid a visit there to see it. Joyce actually got to try it on after pleading with the salesperson and she liked it so much that she bought a blue suede one for herself!

During the show, Joyce got to give Elvis the lei and I gave him a crown. This was before I knew how he felt about his title: "The King." He often decreed that there was only one King and that was Jesus Christ. Sue got her scarf, but didn't have a gift for him. Beverly Mickle, another friend from Atlanta, had given him a pair of giant sunglasses one night and a huge mouse another night. On the night that she gave him the mouse he was holding it while singing "Can't Help Falling in Love" and instead of saying, "Take my hand..." he sang, "Take my RAT..." Too funny!

Each show followed the same basic format, but there were spontaneous songs thrown in, as well as the random feedback from the fans. Even if he was doing the same songs, they were performed differently. With Elvis you never knew what was coming and everyone around him stayed tuned in, so that they would be ready to accompany him wherever he chose to take the song. He

appeared to be in a good mood and responded well to the audience. The more they applauded, the more into the antics he got.

Cameras were not allowed in the showroom in Vegas and we had to be as sneaky as possible to snap these pictures, shooting with high-speed film and using available light only - no flashes to give us away. It's amazing how good these hurriedly snapped photos came out - I always had a lot of luck where Elvis was concerned. We also managed to sneak in mini tape recorders in our purses and place them under the table. I am so grateful for those tapes, as they contain rollicking moments and some pieces of songs that Elvis never recorded, like Dean Martin's "That's Amore," and Chuck Berry's "Hail! Hail! Rock & Roll!" When I met Elvis I told

69

him that I was from Memphis, but currently lived in Atlanta and this night when he sang, "I Got a Woman/Amen," he changed the lyrics to, "I got a woman way across Georgia...." instead of "...way across town..." Then he pointed in my direction, winked and grinned. He may have just been making a play-on-words about the town of Waycross, Georgia or he was teasing with me, but either way, it was certain that he had spoofed the words for my benefit - making a moment that really was just for me. When he went into his stalled airplane imitation, during the "Amen" portion of the number, he referred to J. D. Sumner as the original, "Deep Throat." He marveled at how J. D. could go all the way off the piano keyboard in a low flat. He then turned to Ronnie Tutt and asked, "What's a low flat, Ronnie?" The answer varied from show to show, from a Chinese mud turtle to a platypus.

At the Wednesday midnight show a girl from the balcony yelled for Elvis to throw something up there. Elvis agreed then asked Charlie for a "what not." He took a plastic cup and put a napkin in it, then decided it was still too light, so he asked his stepbrother, David, to bring out a battery. Elvis moved to the edge of the stage, placed the battery in the cup and threw it. He walked back to center stage and complained, "Not only didn't I make it, but I lost a ring in the process. Hey, I'll try something later; I'll get a baseball." Whoever got the ring Elvis accidentally threw off did not offer it back during the show or ever to my knowledge.

Elvis introduced a new song that evening, the beautiful ballad, "It's Midnight," which was well received by the audience. He cut up quite a bit and was upbeat. Someone called out from the audience and asked him how he was feeling. Elvis replied that he was doing okay, he just had a little cold and fever, but the fever appeared to be breaking. He thanked her for asking then related that of the ten guys who worked for him only two of them were with him off stage, because they were dropping like flies. He quipped, "That's why I don't kiss any more girls than I got to. Anyway let me tell you about this song..." He goes on to make up this tearjerker story about its origin. He speaks the first verse as Sherrill Nielson sings it, then they sing together, "Softly." It was

beautiful. He commented about having put band-aids on his fingers to keep his rings on, because he had lost some weight, and a fan asked for his band-aid! Elvis obliged and walked out on the ramp while trying to get it off. She offered to take it off for him and he admonished, "Okay, but don't take my finger." She removed the band-aid, kissed him and sat back down. Her friend remarked, "Good Linda!" This got Elvis' attention. "Linda? Is your name Linda? I know a girl named Linda, but she aint' here. Sheila's here, so we won't talk about Linda!" Then he got so tickled that he could hardly sing. He was doing "Hound Dog" with that fantastic slow ending when someone handed him a crocheted Budweiser hat, which he promptly put on. Pursing his lips, he remarked that he felt like Moms Mably.

At the Wednesday show one of his leather suits began to come apart, due to his shenanigans. He laughingly asked no one in particular, "Who made this suit? 2,500 bucks man!" A girl sitting near the stage loudly remarked that she didn't like the suit at all! Elvis was somewhat taken aback by her tone. "I didn't ask you if you liked it, Blondie. I don't like your hair either." When he tried to introduce J.D the girl continued to heckle him. He turned to her and snapped that he didn't like her attitude! This was a first for me; a girl being unkind to Elvis was unheard of! Elvis continued the introductions and told a story about how he always wanted to be a gospel singer and went to the gospel shows when he was younger. "Can't you just see me up there doing like this..." He moved about wildly as he made animated faces and the audience chuckled along. He commented about seeing J.D. at Ellis Auditorium when he was fifteen and how he never expected to be on the same stage with him. He said that J.D. was like a father figure to him and you could see it. Elvis would hit one of his astonishing notes and he'd eagerly look to J.D for approval, which was always forthcoming.

When he introduced Glen D., he mentioned that Glen does a lot of arranging and wrote music like the ABC's. Elvis said that if he wanted an arrangement for some big number like "Guadalajara," the next morning Glen would have it all written out for every part.

When introducing Charlie he says, "This little guy, who has his own little fan club, his own little group of Keno players, is Charlie Hodge. I met Charlie in the Army. He sings with me, gives me my scarves and water." Elvis put his arm on Charlie's head so that he was facing into his armpit - naturally Charlie fans at it while playing to the audience. Elvis chastised, "Don't do that - I used those Stay Free mini pads... No! I mean Five Day Deodorant pads!" This brought the house down.

Elvis debuted another song, "If You Talk in Your Sleep," written by Red West. Red is a very talented songwriter, having also written

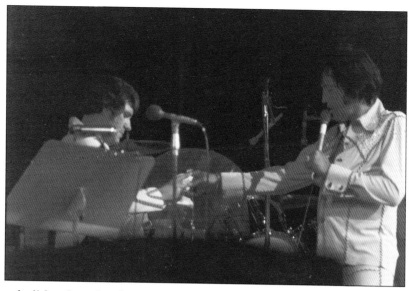

a holiday favorite, "Why Can't Every Day Be Like Christmas," and the touching, "Separate Ways," the song that came the closest to mirroring Elvis' feelings at the time he was going through his divorce and was separated from Lisa Marie. After the song Elvis admitted to some really mischievous prank that he, Red and some of the guys had pulled. For those of you who never went to the Hilton Showroom, there were two statues on each side of a man and a woman, in Louis XIV garb. Elvis wasn't too crazy about them, so Red tied a bucket of paint to his belt, climbed the security fence, stacked up a couple of tables and Elvis and company painted the lady on the left black. Elvis was mystified how no one with the hotel had ever made a peep about it. At this point the Sweet Inspirations began to sing "We Shall Overcome," and everyone broke up laughing. This was all done in a good - humored manner, until someone in the audience called Elvis a "Nigger lover!"

It got deathly quiet as Elvis stood at the edge of the stage to stare down the unseen bigmouthed bigot. "Have you ever looked up that word in the dictionary?" he challenged. "It means shiftless

and lazy and in my opinion there are a lot of white niggers out there!" The crowd stood and cheered for our hero. Elvis had always admired Black music and style of dress; he was tight with B.B King, Sammy Davis Jr., James Brown, Jackie Wilson, and Muhammad Ali, not to mention the Sweets and the Black people that worked for him that he treated like family - he was never a racist.

This incident was followed by a very light version of, "Why Me Lord?" As J.D. would sing, Elvis would make asides. Like when J.D sang "...What have I ever done?" Elvis said, "Too much." J. D. would say "...if I can ever repay..." and Elvis would answer back, "No way!" After the song, Elvis told us about a telethon over at the Landmark where "due to contractual agreements" he couldn't appear. He went on, "So I sent J.D. and the Stamps and two of the Sweet Inspirations, who didn't know any gospel songs! Anyway, it was for a new evangelistic church, so I called up and told them I would give $2500 if the Stamps would all jump into the pool with their clothes on. They did it! When the minister called to thank me I said I'd give another $1,000 if he would jump in! The Stamps ended up throwing the minister into the pool."

Elvis averaged 55 to 75 minutes every show. He explained, "The hotel management don't like for me to appear more than 50-55 minutes, but I get carried away... like the other night when I missed those two shows, because I had the flu. In the whole 19 years I've only missed five shows due to illness. I don't like to miss them. I know people come from all over and I like being up here; it's my life's blood. All of us up here enjoy what we're doing." His caring missive received a thunderous ovation.

This was our last show and Sue had a lei of orchids flown in from Hawaii. When she presented it to Elvis she asked that he place it around Kathy's neck and sing "The Hawaiian Wedding Song." After first giving Sue a kiss and a scarf, he graciously complied with her request. Elvis then left the stage for a moment and changed into his karate jacket. He also put on sunglasses, because his glaucoma was flaring up in the blinding bright lights. He gave a fantastic karate demonstration then introduced his instructor, Master Kang Rhee, who announced that Elvis had just been advanced to an 8th degree black belt. Elvis said he used his karate as good training and discipline, not to be "bad." He earned his first - degree black belt while in the Army and later studied with Chuck Norris and his master, the doyen of American Karate, Ed Parker. Elvis first met Kang Rhee in 1970 at a karate championship match where Rhee was the referee. In 1974 Elvis, entourage in tow, visited Rhee's studio in Memphis. Rhee introduced his students to the legendary star and they demonstrated their skills to him. Elvis later returned and presented Rhee with an autographed guitar and a lion ring. At that same meeting Elvis noticed a young black student standing back shyly. Elvis approached him and handed him a watch saying, "Don't worry about it." That was not the last of the gifts Elvis gave out. Rhee also received a customized Cadillac El Dorado, which replaced his VW station wagon. Kang Rhee

made Elvis a lifetime member of his Memphis Karate Studio. Elvis used to tease Rhee about not smiling enough and Rhee would get on Elvis to keep in shape. They became very close and Elvis even took him throughout the South on tour in 1974. It was indeed an honor to see Master Kang Rhee on the stage with Elvis.

AMAZING GRACE

It was quite an ensemble that traveled with Elvis. Along with his band, orchestra and back up singers, he had roadies and minions, his family and friends, his jeweler, his doctor, his karate instructor, his bodyguards, as well as his consort; right behind him was his following of worldwide fans. Celebrities and big shots were sprinkled throughout his audiences and big stars lined up just like anyone else hoping to get near him. There was also the advance team led by Colonel Parker that hit cities before Elvis did so that they could paper the town and get deejays to play his music and pump the concert. It was not an entourage that merely arrived; it was an armada that landed in waves and took cities by storm. Elvis used to refer to their landings as, "Invasions."

All too soon it was time to return to the real world. We had enjoyed shopping, eating dinner and lunch, with one or more of the group every day and spending the nights being entertained by the master showman, but it was time to pack up our scarves and guitar picks along with great memories and head home, where we would wait with anticipation for our next junket. We didn't have any money and looking back it is hard to believe we were not only able to be there so often, but usually had a nice gift for him as well. We would go three or four to a room and we had a three-letter motto: P.O.R, which stood for, "Pool Our Resources." We were more than friends; we were partners. If one of us had money, all of us had money; it was the only way we could have ever made it work. "Pics - Ticks & Negs;" (Pictures, Tickets and Negatives,) as Phyllis Tate used to say, were what we lived for. We would get the forthcoming tour schedule from Colonel Parker and begin planning our lives to meet up with them out there on the road. We would call our contacts within the group to find out which hotels they'd be at, so that we could be there with them. We'd call the stadiums to see if there were any front row center seats available and if not we used the complimentary tickets that were always available to us. We would start dieting before hand so we could save money and look our best when we got there.

In June mother and I made a trip to visit my Aunt Mary in Memphis. On this occasion I decided to cash in my free admission ticket and visit Elvis at home. My mother and Cousin Sylvia drove me over to Graceland and waited to see me get into the jeep with Uncle Vester and ride up the driveway to the house - evidently there was no statute of limitations on Elvis' offer made to me all those years ago to come by and see him "anytime." It was still another childhood dream come true for me to walk through the front door of Graceland. Linda welcomed me into the living room with another beauty queen, Jeanne Lemay. Linda had given me a phone number to call and said to come on by when I got to Memphis. She was just as sweet as punch, however I stayed in the kitchen and talked Vernon, as I felt out of place around those two stunners. Ricky and David were also there. I can remember hearing them discuss how the only moneymaking business bigger than Elvis was religion.

Elvis was with Charlie and a few others sitting around the piano in the music room, singing and having quiet time, so I didn't want to intrude. I wasn't there as a fan, I was there as a guest, so I just gave him a wave and smile then sat back and enjoyed the privileged view while listening to the sound of Elvis at home - he never sounded better.

Although everyone went out of their way to be kind to me, I was out of my element and didn't want to overstay my welcome - Elvis' home wasn't a hangout for fans and I was so honored to have been allowed in... I still don't know how or why I was so favored, but I wasn't going to abuse it. I didn't want to disturb him by saying some big "goodbye," so I quietly made my way out the kitchen door that opened onto the carport and headed back down the hill. I stopped a moment to look at the array of vehicles parked back there and in a moment Linda came out the back to ask after me. I told her that I had to go. She wanted to get me a ride , but I told her that I'd get a ride from someone at the gate. She said to come by again anytime and that she looked forward to seeing me again soon... such unbelievable consideration... I went to Graceland on other occasions, and Uncle Vester would open the gates and I would walk around the property, but I would have never gone

inside the house even though Uncle Vester had invited me to, because Elvis already did enough for his fans, me included, and I wanted to be as courteous to him as he had been to me. I only went back into the house one more time and saw Elvis, but by then it was too late to tell him how much I cared, and it is a memory that breaks my heart to this moment.

In December 1974 Joyce and I decided to go to Memphis again, as Elvis would be coming in from the tour. Sue had flown in earlier, so the three of us were at the airport awaiting his arrival. But somewhere between L.A. and Memphis, Elvis changed his mind and ended up going to Colorado. We went to Graceland and talked with Harold and some of the fans. The next day we went to see Mike McGregor, who designed jewelry for Elvis and was one of the finest people. Mike had met Elvis at the western supply store where he worked and when Elvis bought the Circle G Ranch in

1967, he asked Mike to come and work for him, to oversee the care of the horses. Mike was an accomplished leather craftsman as well as a jewelry designer. He made custom leather saddles, tack, leather coats and other wardrobe items for Elvis, in addition to

some unique rings and bracelets done in sterling silver and turquoise. After the ranch was sold, Mike remained with Elvis for quite a while; he lived in back and took care of the horses, before moving to Oxford, Mississippi and opening his own shop, which continues on his memory. I received an obsidian ring mounted in sterling silver from him while I was there on this trip. I didn't have enough money for the ring with me, but Mike insisted that I take it then refused to allow me to send him the balance later.

In 1974 there was a newcomer to the Elvis entourage. Dave Hebler was another karate champion who had studied with Ed Parker and was added on as security. He was friendly and courteous and had a great sense of humor, but was a little quieter than the other guys. He had first met Elvis in 1972, and in 1973 Elvis had sealed their friendship by giving him a 280SL Mercedes Benz, just because Dave helped Elvis score a karate tournament.

1975 proved to be the most exciting year Elvis-wise. Considering that I saw almost every show he performed that year. The whole Elvis-experience was fantastic, because it took us to so many wonderful places, including a trip to Las Vegas with my mother and then onto Hawaii where we stayed at the Coco Palms - one of the locations where Elvis had filmed Blue Hawaii. By now we were friends with most everyone in the group. Red, Sonny, Lamar, Dick, Joe, Jerry, and Felton. Jerry Schilling was obviously in love with Myrna of the Sweet Inspirations. (They later married and divorced) Felton Jarvis was alive because of Elvis. He needed a kidney transplant and Elvis had taken care of the expenses. Dick Grob was a former narcotics detective for the Palm Springs Police Department. Joe Esposito had a beautiful wife, Joanie, who was a close friend of Priscilla's. Joe was a very private person that did not mingle as much as the others. Sonny and his wife Judy had a son named Brian. Red's wife Pat also worked for Elvis. There was karate expert Ed Parker who was from Hawaii and not always working on the tour, but was available when needed, and of course Lamar Fike, a mountain of a man before his by-pass surgery, but a gentle teddy bear that was a reasonably good sport about the jokes the guys constantly played on him. Marty Lacker had remained close friends with Elvis since high school, though he no longer made the tour circuit on a regular basis and we didn't know. For a while Elvis' stepbrothers, David and Ricky, were around - Billy was kept on the outside and we about never saw him. They were into street drugs and used Elvis' name in many power plays. I was not very fond of them and found Ricky to be especially obnoxious. Elvis tried to look after them, but sometimes it was quite an effort, according to the stories we heard. Dr. Nick's son, Dean, was along at times. We also became friendly with Tom Hulett and Charles Stone of Concerts West, the agency through whom Colonel Parker booked Elvis' tours. We were close with the entourage, as well as Kathy, Myrna, and the Stamps more than with any of the band members, except Charlie. Of course, we didn't really classify Charlie as a band member; he was more than Elvis' friend, he was family; he was always there near Elvis, close at hand, under his roof, and by his side. Elvis respected Charlie - who is by far the greatest harmony singer ever - and cared deeply for him. He was so comical and a great impersonator; he would have you in stitches with some of his bits. Being Southern as well, we felt right at home with him.

The performers that surrounded Elvis throughout his career were equally talented at what they did; they had to be in order to cover the scope of Elvis' musical vision, which ran the full spectrum of genres. Scotty Moore was the founding father of Rock & Roll guitar solos when he was still with the Starlite Wranglers, and Bill Black brought the spirit of Rockabilly alive with his raucous manhandling of his bull fiddle and D.J Fontana put the rock in Rock & Roll with the stylish way he surrounded the original trio with his creative licks. His back up singers had been the fabulous Jordinares, the most successful gospel group of their era, and for good measure he brought in the incomparable Floyd Cramer to tickle the ivories for him. By the 1970's he expanded his accompaniment and assembled the most incredible stage band ever, bar none. He backed himself with the finest voices - individually and collectively... the most angelic of high voices was contrasted by the man with the lowest voice on the planet. (J.D Sumner is listed in the Guinness Book of World Records for the depth of his basso.) The Sweet Inspirations had been with the "Queen of Soul," Aretha Franklin, before they went with Elvis. The Imperial Quartet had albums that sold well in Gospel circles. They had a fresh vibrant Pop sound that gave Christian music crossover appeal and Elvis had been a fan of theirs even before they worked together. James Burton was another pioneer of Rock & Roll lead guitarists, while with Ricky Nelson, and is a member of the Rock & Roll Hall of Fame. Ronnie Tutt, who is currently touring with Neil Diamond, is the greatest drummer ever; (I don't care what Acid Rock lovers say!) so powerful and yet so much finesse. He even learned karate so that he could follow Elvis' movements and reflect his passions. This is how a great man improves himself, by surrounding himself with greatness. For me it was an incredible experience being around so many exceptional people - you definitely felt like you were in the winner's circle.

Sometimes we accepted the free concert tickets, which bore the initials "EP" where the row number was supposed to be - it was usually Row 10. If we decided at the last minute to attend a show that we didn't have tickets for, we knew we could always get these. Other times, we purchased front or second row seats. At one of the Asheville, N.C. concerts I had gotten tickets from Joe. Sonny had saved me two also. When I saw Sonny after the show he said that he had saved me two tickets but didn't see me. I kept them as a souvenir. It was great being friends with the people that worked for Elvis.

We also met some super fans who were excellent photographers and produced some of the most beautiful, professional pictures

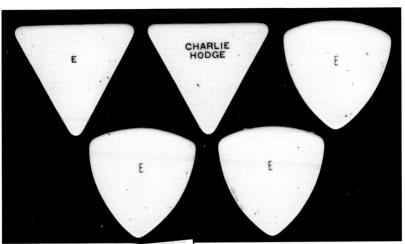

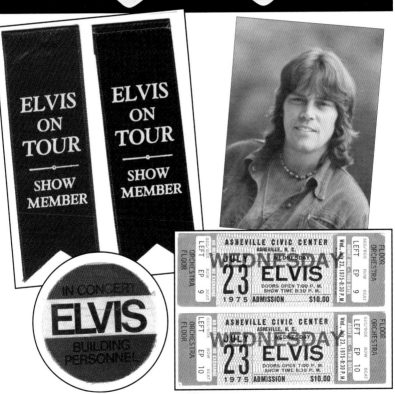

I've ever seen. George Hill, of Panama City Florida, Sean Shaver, who at that time lived in Kansas City and had The Elvis Presley Fan Club, and Keith Alverson, of Atlanta. These men were devoted Elvis fans and friends who never were pushy or tried to rip anyone off. There was also Paul Lichter. While I met Paul only once, and had no problems with him, I had heard rumors that Elvis disliked him because he tried to push his way into the circle and proclaimed to have a closer friendship than actually existed - Elvis didn't like disingenuous people. Once while waiting for Elvis to disembark from his plane in Atlanta the plane was suddenly turned around 180 degrees. We were told that it was because Lichter had been spotted and Elvis did not want to give him the opportunity for pictures. Someone else said it was not Elvis, but the Colonel that didn't like Lichter, because of his success in selling pictures without giving the Colonel his entitled cut. But then Paul told me that he had become very close to the Colonel, and years later he and his son served as honorary pallbearers at the Colonel's funeral. Back then though, there was some controversy surrounding Paul Lichter; ever since then he has been doing quite well selling Elvis memorabilia and books.

There were many fans from all over the world that we met who attended the Vegas shows and the tour concerts that we have unfortunately lost contact with, but will always think of fondly... Christa Trant, Christine Colcolough, Ersie Goins, Wendy DeMarino, Sharon DeThomaso, Len and Rosemary Leech ... the list goes on; all names and faces so familiar, so much a part of those five magical years. We would see each other around the haunts in city after city, where we would always mingle and catch up with each other and exchange Elvis stories. There were cliques and camps, with the usual amount of petty backstabbing and infighting, over jealousy or ignorance, but mostly these gatherings were filled with some of the most loving, caring people I have ever known - Elvis world is still like that overall mo matter how hard that is to believe at times. We were all part of something greater than ourselves and we each felt that we had our own special connection to the man his people and the event, and we were right.

I saw Elvis in Macon, Georgia, Jacksonville, Florida, Tuscaloosa, Alabama, Asheville, North Carolina, Huntsville, Alabama, Charlotte, North Carolina, and Las Vegas during 1975. Each time I saw him, it became more apparent that something was going wrong. His weight would fluctuate at different points of the tour and at times he was lethargic on stage. We were told he was taking cortisone shots for his knee and that the medication for his glaucoma was causing problems. He was in and out of the hospital with reports of exhaustion, colon problems, and pneumonia. My Aunt Mary in Memphis told me that her friend, who was a nurse at Baptist Memorial Hospital, said that he was consuming large doses of prescription drugs. I was indignant at such a remark and vehemently denied it. We knew that he had an elongated colon and had heard rumors that he had the onset of bone cancer. Elvis had legitimate medical problems and these reports were making it sound like he was some drug addict. I became more and more concerned about his health each time I saw him. We all thought that Elvis needed to take more time off between tours, but he wanted to keep touring, because he really wanted to give as many people as possible the opportunity to see him live.

FAME AND FORTUNE

We arrived in Vegas on March 26th and saw eight shows, departing on Easter Sunday. Jackie Kahane was still doing the routine that had gotten him booed off stage at Madison Square Garden back in 1972. Donnie Sumner, Tim Batey, and Sherrill Nielson (who later changed his name to Shaun) had formed a group that Elvis dubbed "New Age Voice," which was shortened to "Voice." The name came from a publication by Larry Geller, Elvis' hairstylist and friend who shared Elvis' passion for theosophy. Voice was now part of the troupe. They opened by singing gospel music then did a number called, "Going Back to Memphis," which was terrific. The Sweets did a fantastic job on Elton John's "Philadelphia Freedom" and Patti Labelle's "Lady Marmalade" then closed with a Stevie Wonder medley. Myrna and I had become friends and I always took pictures of her for Jerry. She had such a cute figure and a beautiful smile; her voice was so pretty and high. But we were there to see Elvis and we were really restless. After his recent hospitalization and so many articles being written about his health, we were anxious for the show to begin, just to see if he was all right.

Elvis appeared onstage wearing a flashy modified suit. It had sparkling fish scales across the shoulders, front and back. There were three suits that were done in this similar style - one in white and navy, one in and orange and navy, and another in navy and light blue. His voice was beautiful and Elvis expended his complete talent on his fans. J.D. had ruptured a blood vessel and his nose was packed, but there he was, in his bedroom slippers, no less, singing his heart out from the bottom of his cavernous vocal cords. From time to time J.D. had to leave the stage due to excessive bleeding, but he'd be back before long...

Somewhere during "I Got A Woman/Amen" Elvis threw his guitar - not backward as usual, but off to the front where it fell with a loud thud. He turned to Charlie and chastised, "You should have caught the son - of a gun; that's the first time you've missed in five years!" Due to it being Easter, Elvis received a myriad of gifts and stuffed animals - after accepting it enthusiastically, he would mostly have these sent to children's wards in the area after the show or he would give them to friends and fans as keepsakes. I gave Elvis a plaque that I had made from a photograph of Graceland that I took myself, and he seemed to like it a lot. He held it up for the audience to see and announced, "This is my house; it's where I live in Memphis." I also gave him a picture of him doing a mean karate kick, which I had taken the previous year when he was much trimmer. When he saw it he shook his head dejectedly and lamented, "Yeah I used to do that. I'm not getting better; I'm getting older - me, and the Sweet Inspirations. Elvis and old women on stage and old Charlie Hodge." Everyone laughed, but it was kind of sad actually; he was too young to be nostalgic over lost youth. We also made a sign that read, "Atlanta Loves You!" He announced that he would be in Atlanta at the Omni in about a month. He chuckled then exhorted, "Omni-hominy-grits!"

One of my all-time favorite songs was the magniloquent, "And I Love You So." Elvis sang this number with so much feeling that it brought tears to my eyes. I loved all the new songs that he was adding to the show; he really kept it all fresh, by singing a range of numbers, like, "The First Time Ever I Saw Your Face," "Promised Land," and "Fairytales." He said that he didn't like to sing "Fairytales," because it was hard to sing. Hard or not, he did a tremendous job on it. However he did not sing it at every show. Wednesday night he did "Steamroller," and Thursday at the midnight show he did "Bridge Over Troubled Waters," for which he received a rousing standing ovation. At the Saturday midnight show a young man jumped onto the stage and grabbed Elvis around the waist. Elvis instinctively drew back to hit him, but Red and Jerry grabbed the man as a hotel security guard jumped across a table to the stage and pulled him away. The young man appeared to be mentally challenged and only wanted a scarf... he started to cry because of all the commotion. When Elvis realized this he grabbed him close and hugged him then said, "Buddy, I'm sorry." He got a scarf and then Jerry took him backstage. When I saw Elvis put his arms around this man my heart went out... this is the main reason I love him so; he was a humanitarian that loved his fans as much as we loved him.

There were a lot of fill-in pieces at these shows, which was unusual for Elvis. Bill Baize of the Stamps sang, "When It's Time For Me To Call On Him," and Sherrill Nielson played piano and sang, "The Hawaiian Wedding Song." Elvis also asked Kathy to sing "Our Heavenly Father." Elvis loved to hear her sing and lavished her with praise. Her voice is truly heaven sent. They were all very talented in their own right, but naturally we wanted to hear Elvis sing, since we had all traveled so far and spent so much to be there. Elvis explained that he had a lot of talented people onstage, so he may as well use them so that he can rest. It was obvious that he was not up to par on this leg of the tour, but he still had some glorious moments.

Jerry Scheff had temporarily left the band and was replaced by Emory Gordy from Atlanta. Gordy had done session work for Elvis

in March of 1972, sitting in for Jerry Scheff on "Separate Ways," "Burning Love," and "Always on My Mind." When Elvis needed someone to take Scheff's place on the tour circuit, he chose Gordy who lasted until September 1973. Gordy was replaced by Duke Bardwell from Baton Rouge. Duke had met Ronnie Tutt on a session for Jose Feliciano and Ronnie recommended Duke to Elvis. Every night when Elvis did the introductions he teased Duke unmercifully, saying that when he was three years old he could play a broom better than Duke could play bass, and wanted to know how could Duke follow an act like Ronnie Tutt. (Duke was introduced after Ronnie did his thundering drum solo.) Finally one night after Duke finished playing his intro piece, he did a humorous soft shoe and Elvis cracked up. Bardwell stayed with Elvis until Scheff's return in 1975. This was also when David Briggs took over piano from Glen Hardin. Elvis took David's denim hat and put it on saying, "Lay some jive on me, man." Linda Thompson's name would later be linked romantically to Briggs.

One night before the show I was seated in a booth with Kathy Westmoreland, who had a date with a black man, and also Myrna and Jerry with there with Mryna's son. Joe Guercio walked over to the booth, looked at the two mixed couples and probed, "Don't you have your dates mixed up?" Then he just laughed and walked away.

Lee Majors was working as a bodyguard for Elvis and wearing a TCB necklace. When Elvis introduced Majors onstage he told the audience that Majors wouldn't let his wife, Farrah Fawcett, have a TLC necklace. His exact words were, "He wants a TCB, but he won't bring his wife around me... he married the girl who does the shampoo commercials. I hate him!" Elvis actually had Majors move in slow motion as he did on the "Six Million Dollar Man." He did his pantomime run to the edge of the stage threw a scarf he had around his neck into the crowd then kissed a few girls! Elvis cracked, "See how fickle those girls are!" Between shows Phyllis Tate and I were introduced to Majors when we happened upon him talking to Red West; Majors was wearing a black sweater, black jeans, a black watch cap and sunglasses! He obviously didn't want to be recognized, but I'm afraid I didn't help him in his quest for anonymity. Once we realized who he was, I was quite excited and started to babble. Red looked at me like I had just landed from Mars, then started laughing, because I never acted that way around Elvis. But Elvis was home folks. I never thought of him as a star, even though I remained in awe of him. But in my mind he was still that guy who had endearingly put his arms around me that summer of 1956. But Lee Majors! I still cherish the autograph he gave me that night signed, "Love, Lee Majors." Fortunately he had never been sued by a crazy woman.

Among the celebrities who attended Elvis' shows while we were there were Cary Grant, Barbara Streisand and her husband, Jon Peters, The Righteous Brothers, Don Adams, Tom Jones, and Tanya Tucker. One night Billy Swann was there and Elvis taunted, "Hey Billy, I just recorded 'I Can Help' and I'm going to blow you right off the charts, man. Naw, just kidding; stand up Billy." We met him, Don Adams, and The Righteous Brothers after the show and got their autographs too.

It was at this time that Streisand and her husband were meeting backstage with Elvis and the Colonel about merging to remake the classic motion picture, A Star Is Born. For a while Elvis was very excited about the prospect and it seemed like he was going to do it, but in the end the details could never be worked out sufficiently. He was very disappointed about not playing one of his favorite roles. The Colonel didn't like that it was basically "Barbara's movie," produced by her husband, and she'd get top billing. (As had Janet Gaynor and Judy Garland respectively when they played the role.) Colonel Parker also didn't cotton to the idea of Elvis playing the role of a has-been, drugged out, washed-up actor that kills himself. The Colonel thought of Elvis' image first and didn't believe that his fans would want to see him that way. Still it would've been quite a coupling to hear the preeminent vocalists of the era meld artistically.

So much wrongheaded criticism has been leveled at the Colonel, for his deals and business practices, when there is much credit due to him that he is denied. It's strange to me that over the years people have tried to lay blame on Colonel Parker for his successful marketing of Elvis. I wish that writers would stop telling the story of Elvis & Colonel Parker like their relationship was based on deceit and was an artistic failure, when in fact it was the most successful partnership in entertainment history and one that is still going strong. "Show Business," are two separate yet equally important words. Elvis took care of the show and the Colonel took care of the business , they were two halves of a whole, partners, and they sliced the pie down the middle. Colonel Parker had all the necessary connections when they met and Elvis had all the needed talent, so they agreed to split the take between them. Elvis was making fantastic records that created a stir for over a year before Colonel Tom Parker came into his life, but they weren't selling millions of copies and playing nationally then worldwide. He had just as much talent when he made $18.00 on the Louisiana Hayride to play for a radio audience of thousands of Mid Southerners, as he did when he performed on "The Ed Sullivan Show," a year later, for $100,000 and was seen on television by 1 out of every 1.3 people in the country. (A ratio that will never be broken! That's why T.V Guide chose Elvis as their "Entertainer of the Century," in 2000. They also knew that they could make a half a dozen different covers with his face and sell them all out.) Colonel Parker obviously never did anything to hurt Elvis' career and certainly had an unbelievable track record for success. Elvis was playing picnics and opening up supermarkets, sometimes doing gigs in the same day in cities that were a couple of hundred miles apart across state lines. Deejays were hardly playing his music, because it didn't fit any known format and Elvis, Scotty, and Bill were selling records out of the back of their jalopy. The Colonel came along and changed all of that, cashing in his promise to Elvis that he would turn his million dollars worth of talent into a million dollars in one year! Twenty years later the scope of their empire was boundless.

What astounded me to think of were all the people that derived their living from the sales of Elvis Presley's amazing talents. He created mass industry, from RCA plant workers and executives, and the people in the MGM division that exclusively handled his movies, to the recording studio engineers and musicians and concert promoters. There were lawyers and private detectives always on the clock, agents getting fees, worldwide distributors making commissions, not to mention an unbelievable legitimate and bootleg retail souvenir industry. There were merchants and providers that made their living off Elvis as practically their sole client. He bought out department stores, clothiers, furniture shops, car dealerships, and grocery stores, because somebody always needed something. He fed, housed, clothed, and cared for a legion of personal staff members that took care of him and his homes. They all dressed in sharp outfits, wore plenty of jewelry, drove expensive flashy cars, and lived well, enjoying the best of everything - so did their families. There were the salaries of the band, the orchestra, and the backup singers, plus there was the cost of their travel and upkeep on the road. They not only traveled around together doing gigs, but he'd take them all on vacation with him and pick up the tab for everything - A-1 treatment all the way. He maintained several mansions, for himself as well as for Priscilla and Lisa Marie. He bought houses and condos for many of those close to him - family, doctors, jewelers, bodyguards, fans and servants. He gave away jewelry and luxury cars like they were loaves of bread, armed everyone around him with complimentary weapons, doled out charity and handouts and loans that were never repaid, to any and all who asked, while keeping several of his ladies and their families living in comfort. Elvis was always picking up the hospital bill when his people got ill or had babies - always the best medical care money could buy for his people. Then there was Vernon and his wife and her three children living in a luxurious home with all the fixings of wealth, and when they were divorced Elvis had to buy Dee off with a huge alimony settlement. There were family living on the grounds at Graceland, and Grandma Minnie Mae had a room downstairs from Elvis - Vester, Harold, and Travis all had nice homes around the corner.

Of course this was all a backdrop to Elvis' buying sprees that included an armory of weapons, a vault of precious stones, costumes that were so expensive they were insured, a warehouse of splendid clothing, and a fleets of cars, bikes and contraptions. If he found something he liked he'd buy several of them, so that others could experience the joy with him. Soon enough he'd give his away and be onto something else exquisite. When he gave you something it was really yours. Some wealthy people lease cars in the company name for their subordinates as a write off, or own homes for corporate tax shelters and the people living there are merely squatting until the asset is liquidated. With Elvis, the deeds and titles were in the name of the beholder. He assembled his own air force when he purchased the Lisa Marie for his personal use and bought the Colonel a Jet Star named Hound Dog. Elvis used the planes like a taxi service to bring him the people and products that he desired in a flash. He thought nothing of spending tens of thousands of dollars to send the plane off to Indiana for sandwiches or take Linda's sickly dog, Gitlow, to Massachusetts to be treated by the best vet in the country. Let's not forget that all of this spending began only after the IRS took its unbelievable gouge from the highest individual taxpayer in the country. Then there was the unprecedented 50% managerial fee extracted by Colonel Tom Parker who spared no expense on his lifestyle. He was losing millions a year on the gaming tables in Las Vegas, but he didn't care, because he had money to burn. It didn't matter if he won or lost, he just loved to play the game. And why not? Like Elvis he had earned it to spend it how he pleased.

POT LUCK

On April 24th the madness started again, this time in Macon, Georgia. Phyllis Tate and I drove there for the wonderful opening show. Elvis wore the navy blue suit with sparkle on the shoulders and down the pants. He looked a little shaky to me; he was pale and sluggish, but his voice was great, and he received many standing ovations. We had front row seats and again got kisses, scarves and winks from Elvis. We couldn't hang around afterward, because we had to drive to Jacksonville, Florida for the next night's show. We met Joyce there and went to the Hilton hoping to see Elvis, but he went out another way. We raced over to the coliseum just as the drums began. Elvis this time was wearing the white suit with the swirling blue design on the shoulders and down the pants. We were in the second row, dead center, which was a great vantage point for pictures. We made eye contact with him a couple of times, but we didn't try to get a scarf or approach the stage. He did his new hit Country & Western single, "T-R-O-U-B-L-E," which really got the crowd going. The people in Jacksonville went absolutely berserk! He could do no wrong. They loved everything and anything that ELVIS did. I guess this made up for the night in '56 when he only got to wiggle his little finger for them. He left immediately after the show and headed for Tampa. We went to my mother's house at Jacksonville Beach to get some rest then made tracks for Atlanta, because Elvis was coming to town for three more shows.

April 30th in Atlanta brought more excitement. Earlier there had been a parade in front of the hotel, which included floats depicting several Elvis movies, local deejays giving testimonials, and a Miss Georgia Universe smiling and waving. It seemed that all of Atlanta had turned out to cheer for the coming of Elvis. That evening he wore the same white suit with the blue trim that he had on in Jacksonville. I had a TCB made of flowers on a chain and

also a framed picture of him with his first grade class that was given to me by Rosemary James. I wasn't happy with the TCB at all, but it had set me back pretty good penny, so I decided to give it to him anyway. He came down to the edge of the stage after he had completed "I Got A Woman/Amen," then looked at me and invited, "Come on, baby." I excitedly made way to the stage and casually leaned on it waiting for him to come to me. The whole place went wild! First I gave him the flowers... he looked a little puzzled, until he realized what they were supposed to be and then he smiled broadly. He got down on one knee and put a blue scarf around my neck and that's when he saw the photo. He took it, studied it a moment, grinned, kissed me and exclaimed, "Thanks honey." I floated back to my seat smiling all the way; I was the envy of the room! Joyce gave him a flower lei, which had become her signature gift, and received the coveted scarf and kiss from our guy.

One night up in his suite, these girls openly admired Elvis' bracelet and ring, so he took them off and gave them away for the asking! Joyce and I thought that we would be conspicuous in that we never asked for anything, and hoped that Elvis would notice this noble trait and give us something for not asking for anything. Wrong! But then again, those girls hadn't been to his home or received in person within his realm by his people, so on the whole, what we had was much more valuable... but hey, we just would have loved being given a brand-spanking-new Cadillac convertible so that we could drive to his shows in style is all. It was a great first night and we left around 1 am anxiously anticipating the next night's show. Well you couldn't imagine my surprise when the following morning, there was Elvis kissing me right on the front page of the Atlanta Journal in a photo taken by photographer Bud Skinner. (Cover Photo version by Sean Shaver.)

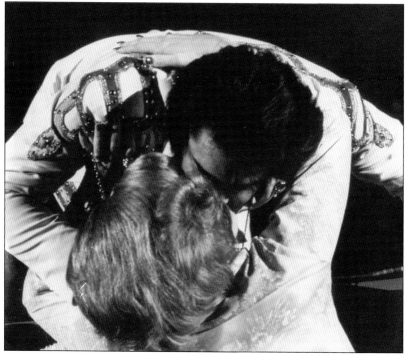

The next night Elvis had on the blue suit that he had worn in Macon. I had a flower guitar for him and once again early in the show he motioned me to the stage. He clowned around with it a bit and then gave it to Charlie. He gave me a warm kiss and thanked me sincerely. I don't know what it was, but everyone, from my friends to my husband, noticed that Elvis mostly gave pecks to some of the ladies, but would really plant one on me. It was a fantastic experience! His breath was so sweet and if it was early enough in the show you could smell the Brut cologne on him. His face and hair and lips were wet with sweat and you were engulfed in his steamy aura for a delightful moment before contact. I would wrap my arm around his neck gently and brush my hand against his soft fine hair. He was the world's greatest kisser without a doubt and had kissed a plethora of women, so I would do my best to hold my own during the kiss. I would gently press my lips against his as his nose went to the side of mine and touched my cheek. When it was over the best part was making that scintillating eye contact that spoke volumes. I had many wonderful exchanges with Elvis, but this was my favorite one with him onstage.

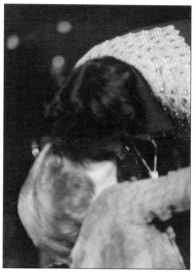

About midway through the show someone threw a pair of polka dot bikini underwear to him, but they missed the stage and fell right at my feet. I picked them up and walked up to the stage holding them out. He looked down at me and wanted to know, "Are those yours, honey?" When I shook my head he got down on one knee and asked, "Well are they clean?" I told him that I had no idea while the audience howled. He laughed at his own mischief then scolded himself. "I gotta quit asking questions like that!" He kissed me again and took the panties from me. Not ready to sit down, I asked him for his guitar pick, which he handed to me then gave me still another kiss! The audience was going crazy and I loved spending a special moment in his spotlight. It was another fantastic show. We didn't go back to the hotel this night - I don't remember why, but there must have been a good reason.

At the final show, Elvis wore the same white suit that he had worn the first night. I didn't find those suits very appealing, but Elvis seemed to like them and so did many of the fans. I had a big flowered heart made for him this night. I don't know why I did flowers all the time. I didn't do them after this night because some girl pointed out, "He's not dead you know!" I never connected the flowers with funerals; so many girls gave him roses I thought something symbolic in flowers would be nice, but her comment changed my mind. Anyway, I'm sitting by Phyllis Tate and fidgeting with the gift on my lap when she punches me and says, "Go! He's motioning for you." I jumped up like a shot and then realized it was not a song he usually interrupted to interact with the audience. He was already at the back of the stage, facing the fans in the balcony, so I thought I was too late, but when he saw me, did a double take, and came right to me. He got down on his knee, took the heart, kissed me, gave me a white scarf and queried, "I guess you want the guitar pick, too?" I grinned and nodded, and he pressed it into my hand with a wink and a smile.

When I got back to my seat I told Phyllis that I was going to kill her, but she assured me that it worked out great; she was very excited for me and so was I. Next, Dorothy Campbell gave him a book on antique cars and he looked at it quizzically, "Antique cars?"

She replied, "I wanted to give you something different." He nodded and gave her a scarf and a kiss. Joyce had another lei for him, which he had come to expect from her by then I'm sure. He put it on and showed his appreciation to her. Strangely enough we never compared notes about these magical kissing experiences. Those who hadn't been fortunate enough to have received one of his prized kisses would ask us about it, but beyond smiling and confirming how sweet it was, we didn't elaborate. In spite of the public forum in which they were given these kisses were private, between you and him.

Once again it was a fabulous evening. "American Trilogy" received a standing ovation throughout the entire song and it was such an exhilarating shared experience that it bonded everyone there. He left immediately after the show bound for Monroe, Louisiana. These shows in Atlanta were incredible and Elvis sounded great. I was a little concerned about his appearance, but he seemed to be in good spirits. I hoped that maybe he was getting

better and he would take an upturn professionally, physically, and personally. Elvis was the kind of person that you instinctively cared about, because you knew how caring he was. His whole family was that way and it was passed onto the people around him. Every experience I'd had with Elvis and his family and his people had been a monument to kindness, from Mrs. Presley's lemonade to complimentary tickets to shows anywhere he was. His Cousin Harold looked after my son for me and let him open the fabled gates for "The Boss." When we were on the tour we'd see the guys around in the restaurants and we'd all get together; they were always picking up the checks, they went out of their way to be so gracious to everyone. When Elvis saw me fall he asked after me, because he cared that I was all right; when we were chilling in the cold car outside the studio, he sent us hot chocolate and invited us in - no one else would have had the authority to let in strangers at one of his recording sessions. Later that night when he saw us at the hotel he worried that we were still up so late. That time on the way to the concert he offered us tickets then allowed us to join his escort, so we wouldn't be late. I had visited him at two of his homes and his hotel suites in several different cities, he had given me autographs, scarves and kisses, and showed me extraordinary down - home hospitality, considering that he was the most beloved singer in the world and I was just an everyday lady with nothing to offer him but my sincere devotion - which he still has. It was amazing that he had these kinds of relationships with so many of his fans and people in his world.

If I gave any portion of that back by being trustworthy and sincere then it was all I could do to repay being allowed a small part of something so priceless. I loved making things for Elvis. He appreciated the thought and was always impressed when people did things that were creative - he'd take the time to make a fuss over you and that was just so very thoughtful of him. Once upon a time Elvis thought enough send along a get well picture to some woman in a hospital that had written to him when she got in a car accident after seeing one of his shows. I can never say enough how thrilling it was for me to receive that gift. Maybe some person that was ill or some lucky fan received one of my tributes and were so excited to have it that they treasured it always. I am happy that I am part of the tapestry. I also wonder if any of those commemoratives of mine are still packed away and catalogued in the massive troves of his belongings. On the E Channel special about Lisa Marie, in 2002, I saw the picture of me handing Elvis that guitar in Atlanta and there was also a picture of Lisa Marie wearing the cap with the crocheted curls that I brought her from Louise as a Christmas gift back in 1973.

We tried to hit all the concerts from the South to the Mid West and of course Vegas. Elvis was appearing in Chatleston South Carolina, Greensboro, North Carolina, Norfolk, Virginia, and Ashville, North Carolina.

After one of the Atlanta shows we had gone into the lounge at the

Hilton with James Burton and some of the others. I was drinking a Bloody Mary and the manager, dressed in a white suit, said that we had to leave because they were closing. As I started to set my drink down James accidentally hit my arm and the drink went all over the manager's white suit. Even though I apologized profusely, we laughed hysterically. One night, Dianna Goodman, a Miss Georgia, came into Elvis' suite barefooted.

There was always something going on, but sometimes incidents arose that put a damper on festivities; particularly if Elvis was in one of his bad moods. In Greensboro we were shocked as he began the introductions by making a crude remark about Kathy Westmoreland. He had made jokes during introductions before, but this was acerbic. They had always been very close, so we couldn't understand why he turned on her; he never had exhibited a cruel demeanor before, so we were perplexed. On this night, he was downright mean. Sensing that she was insulted, at one point he snarled, "If she doesn't like it she can get the hell off the stage!" WHAT WAS GOING ON? Then he introduced the Sweets and made an outrageous comment about their breath smelling like catfish and garlic, which was rightfully perceived by all as a racial slur. The auditorium was suddenly still as Kathy, Estelle, and Sylvia walked off the stage. Myrna remained out of respect to her job. Elvis played up Myrna's not walking off by giving her a ring that he was wearing that cost upwards of $40,000. Poor Myrna was embarrassed by the entire episode and tried to give it back to him after the show. Elvis refused to accept it the first time, but she was later successful in returning it... the next night he threw it away into the audience! This was clearly not the Elvis we all knew and loved. He would never have behaved in such a reprehensible manner - it wasn't in his nature. I remembered back when the man had shouted a racial epithet at Elvis and Elvis put him in his place for his bigotry. It began to occur to me right then and there that his poor condition went beyond his illness; he was changing. It wasn't just his weight; it was his attitude. He was being robbed of a part of himself... the best part of himself.

He went on to perform in Asheville on July 2, 1975, and did some of the best shows of the tour, but for some reason the audiences seemed less responsive and Elvis noticed it. At each show he made a point of saying, "I don't know what they've told you about staying in your seat. It's not me. I want you to have a good time." He never did receive a standing ovation, which he deserved on several songs. He was on stage two hours for the first two shows and an hour and a half for the third show - another out-of-the-ordinary event. Tuesday he wore the Indian jumpsuit with feathers, and for the Wednesday and Thursday shows he wore a new costume, a gypsy-type suit, which was among the very best designs he ever wore. It accented his weight loss as well as highlighted his tan and he looked terrific. The shirts were satin, with full sleeves and a band around the arms. One was white, the other light blue, which brought out his stunning blue eyes! They were topped with a black vest with gold detailing. The pants had an insert on the front, corresponding with the scheme of the shirt, and it was decorated with gold sequins in a flashy style.

On Tuesday, Patti "Conrad" Swann presented Elvis and some of the members of his group with monogrammed boxer shorts with various designs on them. This was a real showstopper. Also at that show Elvis presented J.D. with a 10-carat diamond ring, valued at $40,000, in appreciation for J.D. singing with him. Before singing "It's Midnight," Elvis remarked that it had been written by

Asheville, native Billy Ed Wheeler. Even that didn't get much of a rise out of them.

At the Wednesday show I ran into Beverly Mickle, we both belonged to the fan club in Atlanta and had become close friends. Beverly was a caterer and very artistically talented. She always gave Elvis creative mementos. On this night she gave him a shadow box filled with miniature goodies such as a Pepsi bottle (his preference for cola drink), a wrapper from an ice cream Hunky bar (also a favorite that Linda used to sneak these to him in the hospital) a tiny pair of blue suede shoes, an equally small guitar, motorcycle, teddy bear and several gold records labeled with his song titles, as well as pictures of his mother and Lisa Marie. It was absolutely unique and he Elvis thanked her a great deal. I brought Elvis a picture of Lisa Marie, which he seemed to enjoy a great deal - he gave me an especially loving kiss. He then introduced Vernon, saying how sick he had been in the last six months. Vernon received a standing ovation, but Elvis never did. He asked Vernon what he would like to hear. His response was inaudible, so Elvis shrugged, "I don't know that one Daddy. How about 'Promised Land'?"

On Thursday when he sang, "Shake a Hand," someone gave him a surgical glove stuffed so it looked like a hand! Elvis also did a comedy version of "Little Darlin' " with Charlie wearing a scarf over his head and Elvis singing "la la la la" in a falsetto. After Vernon was introduced on this night Elvis sang "Pieces of My Life" for him. He told the audience, "We have four planes carrying all this equipment to be sure that you, the fans, get the best sound possible. We get our reward by pleasing you." And still he got no standing ovation! Elvis surprised everyone by throwing his guitar to a man on the front row. This was surpassed by Elvis giving away two diamond rings to the audience, copies of his own $16,000 ring, but the audience sat on their hands - except for the recipients of his largesse, who went wild. Those were the strangest audiences; I couldn't figure out why they even came if they were going to act like that. There was a request box in the lobby of the Civic Center and Elvis had Charlie hold it on stage as he picked songs from it. When he announced, "Hawaiian Wedding Song," it received only a smattering of applause and Elvis was visibly disappointed. He said something like, "We didn't do it right; let's do it again."

WHEN MY BLUE MOON
TURNS TO GOLD AGAIN!

I had seen Elvis seventeen times in five months at various stages of his weight fluctuation. In spite of being under constant doctor care, he was obviously ill. One night he would appear bloated and listless and the next night he looked thinner and would be in high gear. Some nights he would electrify the crowd with his performance or he would turn on the charm and humor to tease the audience and mock his image... other nights he lifelessly held onto the microphone running through tunes, mumbling in-between songs or rambling on with stories that were hard to follow. There were more fill-ins and more cancellations.

When August rolled around and it was time to go to Vegas, I wasn't sure what to expect. My mother and I were going from Las Vegas to Hawaii and I wanted to be in Vegas for his opening night show, which was always the best. I was not disappointed. He came on stage to a standing ovation. He was resplendent in the black gypsy costume. He appeared to have lost weight and was playing a new red guitar. He had also asked fifty people to write on slips of paper titles of songs they wanted to hear. The requests were placed in a box and he would draw a slip out and sing the song. He seemed to enjoy this, as it was a break from the old routine. However, he did appear to tire more easily as the show went on.

I have been an Elvis fan since before our first meeting in 1956, I had been following his career since then and seeing him at every opportunity and it has filled my heart with true joy to this moment. I have met some really great fans that I have treasured for years, but on this trip to Vegas I was exposed to people who called themselves fans but behaved in a manner, which disputed their claim. For some reason people expected miracles from Elvis. They didn't allow him to age, to be sick, to gain weight or suffer any of the other human frailties, which effect so many of us. Granted he was the greatest entertainer, but he was also human. These so-called fans could not hear his beautiful voice, because they were too busy heckling him to sing other songs than what he was singing. They continuously made derisive comments about his weight and his movements and it became so bad that Elvis left the stage early.

At the Tuesday dinner show the chain on Elvis' belt broke. He remarked that he had paid $2,500 for the outfit and $1,000 for the belt and then began giving pieces to the audience. Following the introductions Elvis sang, "The Wonder of You," followed by the sacred "How Great Thou Art," which received a thunderous, standing ovation. As he sang "Young and Beautiful" someone in the audience yelled out, "Elvis, you're beautiful!" This brought a round of applause, because he was beautiful as a man and as an entertainer and he deserved all the love the fans have given him over the years... I just wondered how much longer he could go on giving his all to the fans...

At the Tuesday midnight show when he drew "Suspicious Minds" from the request box, he exclaimed, "Good gosh Charlie, give me a scarf and two tanks of oxygen." Two songs later he did "Polk Salad Annie," accented with a fantastic karate display. Elvis then sat down on the stage, exhausted. John Kennedy from Griffith, Indiana shouted, "Hey Elvis, my wife will give you mouth to mouth resuscitation!" To which Elvis responded, "Bring her up!" He laid down, while his wife Emma was helped onto the stage by Charlie; whereupon she got down on her knees and kissed Elvis, receiving a scarf for her efforts.

I had told my mother that there were certain songs where Elvis gave out scarves and I would cue her when to stand up. We ate lunch with Dick Grob that day and Mother had told him how much she wanted a scarf. Now my mother is and was quite a beautiful woman and no shrinking violet. Elvis began to sing a "non-scarf" song and my mother, paying no attention to me, stands up, points to herself and declares, "Memphis Mamma!" I was practically crawling under the table when Elvis saw her. He

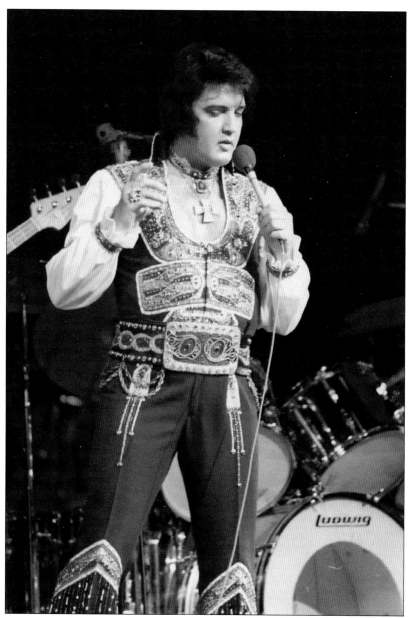

looked at me wryly and walked right over to her. He placed a navy blue scarf around her neck and gave her a kiss. Not satisfied, she asked for his guitar pick, which he gave her. Mother thanked him and he winked at me, shook his head and proclaimed, "Like daughter, like Mother!"

Those were great shows and Elvis had a lot of fun. Beverly Mickle gave him a pair of oversized sunglasses and a frog puppet that he had too much fun with. After the show our friend, Christa Trant, gave him a monogrammed toilet seat that was shaped like a guitar. He quipped, "Now all I need me is a guitar shaped like a toilet seat." Elvis always seemed energized onstage from the audience, the music and the fun and games he played, but once he got offstage and the adrenaline subsided, he was more and more fatigued by his chronic conditions, both external and internal. We left on the third day and Elvis canceled the remainder of his shows due to illness. How glad I was that we had booked the opening show and Mother had gotten to see him, but how sorry I was that he was ill again.

Elvis was back in Las Vegas at the Hilton from December 2nd through the 15th due to the August engagement being canceled after only three days. The hotel tried something different on this occasion, attempting to tie show reservations with room reservations. There were so many complaints that this method did not prevail. Too many fans were staying at other, cheaper, hotels. The promoters worried that spending Christmas in Vegas might not be appealing to his fans and attendance would be low, but our desire to see Elvis knew no seasons or boundaries and once again his sold out shows broke attendance records.

Historically Elvis had always arranged to be off from Thanksgiving until his birthday. He thrived on the holiday season and took great care choosing gifts for the people on his list. It was his favorite time of year and he indulged himself and his family, friends, fans and charities completely. On Thanksgiving, Graceland would be trimmed inside and out with the holiday spirit; lights were strung, decorated trees were scattered throughout the house, and the yard became a winter wonderland. So many of the Christmas ornaments you see today are from the very first noel at Graceland, when he and his momma expended their love for the holidays by making the place into a shrine to Christmas. It was the only Christmas she ever spent there and he clung to those ornaments as a tangible link to her for the holidays. The day after Thanksgiving all the lights were turned on and the house remained decorated until the day after Elvis' birthday, because his birthday gifts were put under the trees. Of all the ceremonies that commemorate him today, this ritual is the only one that fans observe that he enacted himself. Today many Elvis fans pay tribute to Elvis by keeping their tree up from Thanksgiving until his birthday.

On Dec 6, he vexed how he wasn't used to doing a show this early; he virtually got out of bed and walked onto the stage. He sang happy birthday to a lady in the audience, then he sang happy birthday to David Briggs. He got a request for "Sweet Caroline" and when they started it James was in the wrong key. Elvis hollered, "Wait a minute! I know we haven't played it in about 25 years, and everyone's entitled to a stupid mistake, but you're supposed to be one of the best guitar players in the country." Later he ordered Charlie, "Get this red scarf off me; it's itching me to death. Why did we order RED scarves? To match my eyes?" He introduced Colonel Parker and his wife, then Lisa Marie and Vernon. After that he dedicated "Just Pretend" to Mrs. Parker.

Christmas shows always brought unusual and funny gifts from the fans. This year was no exception. Like a child on Christmas morning, Elvis removed toys from a stocking and tried to skate-board across the stage. He tossed a football to Lisa Marie and attempted tricks with a yo-yo. You could just see how much this man-child enjoyed the thrill of Christmas. One gift that was a big hit was a construction helmet with flashing red light on top, and goggles with wipers that Beverly gave him! He laughed so hard he could barely sing, "Love Me," which begins "Treat me like a fool..." How appropriate! At one show Elvis received a sombrero, around which Charlie did a Mexican hat dance. Charlie also did some of his famous imitations, including Gabby Hayes, and Gomer Pyle, which brought the house down. Elvis looked and acted more like his old self and it was a refreshing surprise. He was in a great mood, laughing, kidding and performing in that dynamic manner, so indicative to the renowned Elvis style. Moments like those filled us all with hope that Elvis was going to come around and get back on track; we just knew that he had it in him.

Elvis surprised everyone with booking a New Year's Eve concert in Pontiac, Michigan. Al and Dee Bigelow of the Strictly Elvis Generation Fan Club were instrumental in bringing Elvis there. Their fan club boasted 4,734 members in 50 states and 26 foreign countries. The Bigelows contacted the Pontiac Silverdome in an effort to get them to book Elvis. Elvis liked the idea, but the Colonel wanted to be sure there would be enough interest to sell out the 80,000 seat stadium. He need not have worried. Tickets sold out quickly and at the last minute extra seats were added on the field to accommodate more people at a higher price. The Bigelows hung a banner that read: "Elvis - The Spirit of '76," setting the mood for the concert. This was the largest audience

Elvis ever performed for in person.

This was the concert that Elvis hated the most, wiping out the bad experience he had at the Houston Astrodome in 1970. At show time there was subfreezing weather conditions inside the stadium, because the heating system was down except for inside the concession stands. John Wilkinson joked, "Bring on the dog sleds," but it was no laughing matter. Elvis split his pants in the middle of his first song, but did not find out about it and change his costume until he had completed six songs. The horns were blown off key, because of the freezing temperature, and the echoing acoustics made it difficult for the audience to listen and the band to follow. But Elvis was a trooper and really put on a sensational show for the exuberant fans there to ring in the Bi-Centennial. At midnight the entire stadium resonated with the nostalgic ditty, "Auld Lang Syne." Eight-year-old Lisa Marie as well as Vernon accompanied Elvis to this concert and applauded wildly as he sang "America the Beautiful." At 12:22 am, January 1, 1976 Elvis left the building, got into his car and cursed a blue streak at the conditions of the concert, vowing to never again play in one of those "Space Museums!" Be that as it may, the nearly 1 million-dollar gate was the largest one night take in the history of show business till that time, so the evening wasn't a total loss.

1976 began in typical Elvis fashion, as he gave away nine Cadillacs to the Denver police officers that served as security guards while he and his armada were vacationing in Vail for his 41st birthday. Denver's police medical coordinator, Dr. Gerald Starkey, received a Lincoln Mark IV. When a Denver deejay commented that he wouldn't mind getting a Cadillac from Elvis, he got one too. Also he bought Cadillacs for Linda Thompson and Joe Esposito's new girlfriend, Shirley Dieu. But 1976 would turnout to be a year of profound change in Elvis' life and my own as well. It was the year of the undoing of all that had been before.

Elvis wasn't alone on this grueling touring schedule. Most of his musicians had been with him from the beginning and it was taking its toll on their health and their families. They had been propelled by the thrill of it all for many years, but the tour had since become a grind, because of the relentless schedule and the fact that Elvis was canceling so many dates at the last minute. Elvis' drummer, Ronnie Tutt, and piano player, Glen D. Hardin, left and were replaced by Larry Londin and Jerry Kester respectively. Fortunately this was only temporary and, before the end of the year, both were back, but only off and on thereafter.

Elvis was slipping from his pinnacle during this period and it was hard on those closest to him, and those who were just on the outside, but that said I want to point out that Elvis off his game was far more entertaining than anyone else. Every night throngs of adoring fans overflowed the venues he played at and screamed for him until they fainted. When he was on his game he was incomparable; audiences didn't cheer him, they erupted as a whole and individually succumbed to their excitement. They were driven by their passion for him to do some outlandish things that I'm sure they couldn't believe they had done later, but they were so under his spell that they couldn't help themselves. Despite his weight gain, he was an energetic performer who exploded with a physical fury that was unparalleled. I've seen some great entertainers from the beginning of Rock & Roll right through to this new age of Pop and I respect the dancing skills and showmanship of many, even if I'm not fond of their music or persona, but none of them are nearly as electrifying as Elvis was even during the final stanza of his career, let alone his glory days. What made Elvis so thrilling was that his gyrations weren't based on an impersonal dance technique or even his skilled karate movements, it was his way of acting out each word, so that he bonded with the song; he brought the music to life most vividly with his undulating body, which was singing to us as well, as each note was struck by contorting himself to wring out the dynamic of the sentiment. Other artists have reached this rarefied realm now and then, but no one has sustained it very long. Elvis did it night after night for years in different decades, and poor performances were a rarity, in ratio to how many shows he did... what made the below par performances so glaring is that for years and years he NEVER had an off night... something had to give...

THE SOUND OF YOUR CRY

On March 20th we attended the two shows in Charlotte. Joyce had a front row seat and I had gotten an EP ticket from one of the guys. When Elvis walked out and saw Joyce he chided, "This girl has been from Maine to Spain on a choo-choo train. Honey, do you drive or fly with me?" There were always a lot of subplots going on around edge of the scene and there were pranks, inside jokes, and festivities galore - some of which I'm sworn to keep secret. Red West and Ed Hill were each celebrating a birthday at the time of the Charlotte concert and Beverly and I set about making special birthday cakes for them. Red's wife Pat had joined him on tour and they had requested some privacy, so Charlie took Red's cake back to him. It was a bikini cake with a strategically placed maraschino cherry. Of course we didn't tell anyone about it and Charlie got that piece. He said it was the laugh of the night. I'll never forget that concert, because Elvis put flowers behind his ears and acted like a Flamenco dancing bullfighter.

136

We had been told how to find out a timeframe for their arrival in cities, so that we could be on hand at the airport when they hit town - if we managed to beat them there. We would call the airport and ask if N880EP had filed a flight pattern and they would confirm the information and tell us their E.T.A. (Elvis' Time of Arrival.) So we'd be there to greet him and we'd be there in the front row and if things upstairs were under control, we'd go up and say good night; the perfect Elvis day!

Elvis was back in Atlanta for two shows on June 5th and 6th. Joyce and I had front row seats for both shows, but not together. I was sitting with Sandy Bryant and Phyllis Tate for the show on the fifth. We had been at the Hilton before the show, but for some reason most of the group had not been too visible and we only talked to Larry Strickland and Ed Enoch of The Stamps. Knowing his penchant for clowning on stage, I brought him the head of an old crone. She had a bandana tied over her wispy gray hair and she cackled and spit water when you pulled her string. I knew he would love this funny gift and sure enough he did. He played with her on stage until she ran out of water. Charlie told me later that Elvis thought it was a great gag and filled it up again and again to squirt all the guys. I wonder who ended up with that?

For the next show I did something sentimental and presented him with a picture of Lisa Marie that I had airbrushed onto a plaque. I think he was disappointed and probably wanted something fun to play with on stage again, but he always loved to get gifts that commemorated Lisa Marie and he thanked me warmly - if only I had known that it was to have been our last kiss, I would have ritualized it, but at that time I was looking forward to many more concerts, personal exchanges and kisses from Elvis, so I smiled and drifted back to my seat on cloud nine, as ever. I am just glad that Joyce was there to capture the moment on camera for all eternity. Later, he received a golf hat as well as a pair of glasses, complete with nose and mustache, which he wore for a whole song. He was in a playful mood and was up to great mischief during this engagement; his voice was sensational and his superb range had seemed to gain a new octave. His banter with the group

137

and the audience was engaging and he gave a consummate performance that filled us with pride. I left with a feeling of renewed hope that Elvis was going to be just fine after all. The group was off to Philadelphia and then to Memphis, while I made arrangements to be there on August 31st in Macon. But in those ten weeks the core of his world was shaken to its foundation in ways that no one could have imagined when he took a drastic action that would profoundly alter his life and legacy.

On July 5, 1976, Elvis performed in Memphis for what would be his final time. Twenty-two years to the night earlier, he had taken the town by storm with one little old ditty that played on the radio all night long. The impoverished loner from Humes High had the keys to the city from then on. Twenty years and one day earlier he had performed before my very eyes for the very first time... we had all come along way since then. He spent a typical Elvis-Style 4th of July blowing up fireworks of every kind and driving around the grounds of Graceland receiving kin and hometown friends and being pampered by the staff that loved him and kept his estate ready for his returns. For Elvis, the concert in his own backyard meant he could unwind, sleep in his own bed, and see the moon and stars from the home he loved - it revitalized him. The show was stellar; the press was there to laud him and hail the birth of Rock & Roll, as well as the birth of the nation - there was no greater symbol of the "American Dream" than Elvis Presley!

With some time off between tours, Elvis headed for Palm Springs to get away from it all, and, without a reasonable explanation or proper compensation, he instructed Vernon to unceremoniously fire Red, Sonny, and Dave. That Elvis would let go Red and Sonny - especially Red - was a total shock. Red was such an integral part of Elvis' world; he had been looking out for Elvis since the bullies tried to cut his hair at Humes High School. I would've been less shocked to hear that Vernon was no longer holding the purse strings. Gladys told Red time after time in the early days, "Look after my boy, Red." They had buddied up from Memphis to Hollywood to Germany and back and out to Las Vegas and places all over the map, living on squirt gun fights, fireworks wars, pie throwing skirmishes, shaving cream battles, dodgem car scrums, and practical jokes, while roughhousing and womanizing all the way. We really thought it was another of Elvis' temper fits and that everything would be back to normal by the time of the next tour, but it wasn't to be. Red, Sonny, Jerry, Dick, and Joe were the most important members of the Memphis Mafia, because they were the ones that cared for him the deepest, but Red and Sonny had been

doing it the longest. The bodyguards were entrusted with the life and safety of the most beloved entertainer in the world; they were sworn to die to protect Elvis or avenge his death by executing his assassin. Arguments, fallouts and misunderstandings had occurred over the years between them, but that couldn't negate the heavy - duty bond they shared; these guys were brothers. Jerry Schilling had quit and come back several times and there were no hard feelings. Elvis had fired the guys many times over the years, but after a few days or hours it was all forgotten and the highjinks picked up right where they had left off. We were certain that these men were too important for Elvis to simply discard - how many people can you find to take a bullet for you? But we were wrong and soon realized that the boys wouldn't be back. Al Strata came onto the scene, Linda's brother, Sam Thompson, took over as head of security, the Stanley boys were more involved, Ed Parker came onboard fulltime, and even hairdresser Larry Geller was pressed into security duty onstage - Elvis had moved on.

The last time I had any contact with the group while on tour was after the Macon, Georgia evening show on August 31. I went back to the hotel afterwards and talked with both Jerry and Felton. This night I brought a mirrored jewelry box with, "The Boss" lettered in gold across the top - it was my favorite gift for him. It was too large for me to give to him on stage, so I waited to present it to him in person up in his suite after the show, but he wasn't seeing anyone, so I left it with Felton. I told Felton and Jerry that I had some personal things to take care of and would not be around for a while. I also told them I thought Elvis needed to take some time off and get himself together. It was hard to sit out front clapping to the music when I so worried about him. I asked them if they couldn't talk him into resting for a few months. Felton replied that Elvis wanted to hit as many cities as he could, so that as many fans as possible could see him.

There were more and more reports of him checking into the hospital for exhaustion and canceling shows; it was apparent that the road was catching up with him. I was sure that all he needed was a chance to relax and recuperate and he'd be fit as a fiddle and right as rain - he'd rebound and show them all like he had so many times in the past. He was still an incredible performer, playing to sold-out stadiums overflowing with cheering fans and he continued to expand his range and repertoire, but as great as he was, I knew he was below par, because of his ailments. Why wouldn't he just take a rest for awhile? He had to know that we'd be waiting for him, just like we did while he was away in the Army. It wasn't age, he was wearing out and I was worried to the brink of crying for him; I could feel his pain, because it was so great. Elvis' health was the leading topic among the insiders, but after what happened to Red and Sonny and Dave, no one nagged him enough to get him to change his ways and he was on his own.

Linda was his last hope. She had always been a great influence on Elvis, but even she couldn't force him to take better care of himself anymore. After awhile she became disheartened with everything, and it was a shame to see her great love fading; at some point she realized that he was beyond her loving care - she was dedicating so much of herself to Elvis and his needs that she was empty. Once in Las Vegas, Linda had asked us to have dinner with her and explained that not always having friends or family around and remaining somewhat secluded with Elvis, she was glad to have a friendly face or two to sit down and talk to; particularly people who lived outside the claustrophobic bubble of her insular world. After seeing her with Elvis for so long, we knew how deeply she truly cared for him; the man not the Superstar; not the entertainer, but the human being inside. How sad that toward the end of 1976 Linda had become so disenchanted with the lifestyle that she bid a fond adieu to the love of her life. Even though she remained a faithful and close friend, she would no longer be his love interest. It wasn't the same on the tour anymore with so much of the old gang gone; Elvis' world seemed to be falling apart a piece at a time and no one had any idea how to put it back together.

At the stroke of midnight of the New Year of 1977, Elvis was on stage in Pittsburgh performing his heart out, in high gear and in rare form. He added new songs, brought back some old favorites and rearranged his classics. He was up to his old tricks, and his fun loving stage presence sent joy rolling through the audience, which came back to him in waves of love. He kept the house on the edge of their seats all night with his music, his remarks, and his dynamite moves. Before his closing theme and vamp he sat at the piano and in a soaring voice without a roof performed, "Rags to Riches," which kept the hysterical screams going right on through until he left the build and headed home for a two-month vacation, which is just what the doctor ordered.

Graceland always uplifted his spirit, because he felt closer to his momma when he was there; in his heart it would always be her home. He got to get some home cooking, go on shopping sprees, and rent out the movie theater till dawn. He enjoyed playing racquetball on his private court, slipping out to cruise his new three-wheel motorcycle, and visiting with fans at the gates informally. He had several new romantic interests and a few blasts from the past that came around after Linda was gone, but he had declared his love for 21-year-old Ginger Alden, who looked like a pale version of Priscilla. He took her down to Tupelo to show her where it all began, which meant he was serious about her at that time - so did the 94-carat diamond engagement ring she sported.

Rather than go to studios anymore, the studio came to him, so that he could record in the privacy of his own Jungle Room. He was given some tremendous material that became instant classics. He also had a slew of his oldies albums and 45s achieve Gold or Platinum status that year and awards of recognition for his over 600,000,000 worldwide sales were bestowed upon him from all parts of the globe. CBS signed Elvis to do a concert television special that would be filmed during his summer tour and aired in October - the tour would also be recorded for an album. The special would air as Elvis opened up the palatial new showroom at the Hilton Hotel, which could rightfully be called, "The House That Elvis Built." He was even talking about producing and starring in his own movie where he would play a veteran C.I.A agent working undercover to uncover evildoers.

Despite coming off the most stressful year of his life and career since 1958 then turning 42, Elvis was on the rise and it looked like that he was not only going to be just fine, he seemed primed for another one of those momentous career surges that would send his star streaking across the sky in a blaze of glory that only he could conjure.

Elvis went back on the road in February and I caught up with him in Florida, seeing him in St Petersburg and Orlando. He was in great voice and was very energetic on stage. He often used Charlie to perform his karate demonstrations on and I swear that the two of them were as funny as any comedy duo. His hair was much fuller than it had ever been and he looked good in his Native American style white jumpsuit that was trimmed with turquoise and gold. I didn't take any pictures, because of my poor vantage point and I couldn't get near the stage to go up to him. I could feel the absence of Red, Sonny, Dave, and Linda; even Vernon was too ill to make the tour. There was hardly time to visit with any of the remaining group after the shows, because I was on my way to my mother's house in Jacksonville and they were off to do a series of one-nighters across the Southland.

However at the end of this short tour he was aching from head to toe and completely drained. He suffered from high fevers and intestinal problems and he needed extended bed rest. Even though he was under constant care by several physicians, most notably Dr. Nick, and checked into the hospital regularly, he wasn't getting any better. He cut short a vacation to Hawaii, because he felt so bad. Then he cancelled the remainder of his next tour after only a couple of shows, so along with the scheduled concert dates, he was booked to makeup these missed performances. The plan was for him to do two shows a night for two weeks then take two weeks off, so Elvis hit the skies and spent half of the next twenty weeks hopping from city to city, to give his fans the thrill of a lifetime.

By this time I had set the wheels in motion to leave Atlanta and move to Louisiana. I had a target date of April 1st and hoped to have all my plans worked out by then. I had hardly been on the tour for six months, and I really missed it. I had so many friends out there and we had been such a part of each other's lives that I had a sense of loss. Though Elvis was far away, his records were there for me and I again turned to him in my heart to get through my difficult times. Once I had settled into my new routine I would get back into the swing of things. Then in May I heard that Elvis would be in Baton Rouge doing a make-up show and I got that old excited feeling again. On the 31st I went to the Hilton and did not see even one person I knew, not a fan or any of the group. I called J.D.'s room, but he didn't have any tickets and didn't know where Joe or Dick were. With Sonny and Red no longer working for Elvis, and not being able to find anyone else, I had to go hunt for a lousy seat at a premium price; it was a strange feeling to buy a ticket from someone out in front. I sat in the first row of the side section, way back from the stage. A rarity for me; no front and center seat and no EP seat...

I sat there and listened to all of Jackie Kahane's old jokes and enjoyed the Sweets and The Stamps warm up act. Then the lights dimmed as the orchestra played a Disco oriented version of "2001 A Space Odyssey" the familiar thunderous tom-toms and kettle-drums kicked in the opening vamp and, as the world's preeminent entertainer strutted onstage to the delight of his multitude of fans, my eyes filled with tears and I wept openly... not the tears of old that sprang from excitement and anticipation, but tears of sorrow and frustration. I couldn't believe that it was, him. Thousands of flashbulbs popped continuously throughout the performance capturing his sluggish movements and listless countenance, but I didn't take even one picture; I couldn't lift my arms to photograph him in this condition. I wasn't being critical of him to be judg-mental; hell the best of us can get fat. It wasn't just that he looked out of shape; he looked unhealthy. He didn't seem tired; he seemed out of it. He didn't have command of the stage and was incomprehensible when speaking. He forgot the words to songs then cut them short, but the crowds shrieked with excitement just the same as they always had. He did not drop down in a graceful karate stance and contort his body to greet and kiss the fans near the stage, it was a visible effort for him to get on a knee and lean over, but still they lined up twenty deep to clamor and clutch for him - it was like we were watching two different concerts. To me it seemed that the band was tense. I was attuned to the looks that went back and forth and I could tell that they were worried about Elvis. I didn't look for anyone after the show; I wouldn't have known what to say. I just got in my car and drove back home, crying all the way, broken-hearted.

THE LAST FAREWELL

I have wondered so often if any woman could have helped Elvis when he needed to turn to that special person when he felt alone, bored or just plain fed up with his lifestyle. He never found that one person to love him unconditionally like his momma had and he searched in vain to find another kindred spirit. The immature young waif that he was involved with was in way over her head and neither understood his world, nor cared for him adequately. In all the years of seeing him with one or another of his girlfriends no one had touched his heart enough to make a difference - although Linda had come very close. She had cared for him in every sense of the word, but could not go on. Maybe no one could have made a difference, because Elvis was determined to be ELVIS and there wasn't enough room for anyone else to grow with him... if not Linda, I couldn't imagine who could have made it for the long haul and stayed with him till the end.

In early June he was touring the Mid-West, with the CBS crew in tow capturing every moment on stage. Due to a scheduling conflict, Larry Londin filled in as drummer for Ronnie Tutt, which was too bad, because, while Londin was very good, there was no one who could touch Ronnie Tutt; he had a magical rhythm that really accented Elvis' music and it would be missing on the special and on the album. The tour finished up in Indianapolis on June 26th, and then he would be off for eight weeks between tours. His next concert date wasn't scheduled until August 16th in Portland, Maine. Even a couple of months off wouldn't be enough for him to get himself back together, but maybe he could rest and at least get better. I didn't care if he ever performed again; all I wanted is for him to be healthy and content in his life. He had given his fans more than we could have ever hoped for and it was time for him to take time away from his career to replenish himself.

For a year I had been worried about his condition, but did I

148

think that he was going to die? Of course not, he was ELVIS, and ELVIS doesn't die... certainly not as a young man with a full life and career ahead of him. My concern was that he was suffering from his many ailments; I felt sorrow, because he was assailed with pain. So when the phone rang at my boutique on that mid-August afternoon and my employee, Jeanie Davis, called and told me that she heard on the radio Elvis was dead, I didn't believe it. There had been erroneous reports like this in the past, so I paid it no heed. After assuring her that it was a mistake I had a thought that gave me a chill; "What if it were true?" I hung up with her and immediately dialed Graceland; it was busy. I called the gatehouse; it was busy. I dialed the Los Angeles answering service and was told that they were not taking messages for anyone in the Elvis group. I called Joyce; it was busy. I dialed her several more times and finally got through; she answered the phone sobbing uncontrollably... Elvis was gone! Before breaking down I told her that I would be on the next flight to Memphis and we arranged to meet at the gates.

It was a madhouse in Memphis from the airport to the mansion. The cab let me off four blocks from Graceland due to the crowds, which had spilled into the streets. There were vulgar displays of greed exhibited by coldhearted vendors hawking memorial t-shirts. The crowds were, for the most part, orderly, numbed by grief - still hoping against hope that this was just a nightmare and we'd all wake up and go see him in concert. The stifling heat had people passing out on the sidewalks that were carried to the first aid stations set up inside the gates on the hillside. Old friends that had embraced at concerts around the country greeted each other with tears and sobs and hugs - we were inconsolable. Restaurants were filled to capacity and voices were subdued as people choked back tears. I trudged through the tidal wave of people, finally seeing Sue McCasland. As we collapsed into each other's arms a news reporter tried to take our picture, however Judy Linhard stepped in front of us and told him that it was personal. I continued making my way to the gate, where true to her word Joyce waited for me.

The general public would be allowed to view his body from 3:30 to 6:30 that day; hardly enough time for the nearly one hundred thousand people gathered outside the gates and lined around the block. Uncle Vester was at the gates along with Fred Stohl and when the gates opened to let in a floral truck we were waved inside. We offered our condolences to the uncle that had seen him come into the world, who was heartbroken to see him gone before his time. He hugged us and told us to go on up to the house to see Elvis one final time and say our goodbyes. As we started up the driveway, Jerry saw us and came right over to put his arms around us. I stammered apologetically about how I wasn't trying to put him down the last time we had spoken, I was just so worried about him, but Jerry comforted me and assured me that Elvis knew that we had loved him and he had loved us just as much. Then he asked if we were ready to go up to the house.

We made our way along the driveway and it grew eerily quiet. I could no longer hear the cries from the street of the mourning fans. My heart was thudding against my chest like it wanted to breakout and my stomach was churning. The tears were falling silently until we reached the front porch and then I dissolved. There in the foyer of the pulchritudinous manor, lay the still figure of the most beloved entertainer the world has ever known, a man I had met over twenty years before and cared about very deeply. I crossed the threshold and placed my hand on the copper coffin. I kept my eyes averted at first, not wanting to see the truth, but I finally took one last look and my heartbreak was complete. As Joyce and I stood there with Jerry between us, I suddenly felt like I was watching someone else go through all this. His black hair bore stark contrast to his white suit and his pale visage picked up the hue of his light blue shirt; I could hardly grasp what I was seeing. I half expected him to jump up and start laughing, but he was beyond this world... I looked upon the serene countenance of the man who had brought so much joy into so many lives... as my Elvis lay eternally still before me, I prayed that he found the peace that eluded him in life then I rejoiced that he was again with his momma. It occurred to me that this was the most private moment that I'd had with Elvis since it all began on another sweltering Memphis day decades ago when a friend and I went to see him at his house... I looked away and sobbed loudly for my personal loss, as Joyce crumpled at our feet. How dare she make me focus on her at a time like this! I wanted to devote all my being at that moment to grieving for this man of compassion and love that was lost to us forever. But she was doing the best she could under the tragic circumstances. As Jerry and I struggled to help her to her feet, a paramedic rushed over with smelling salts, then they took her to the ambulance that was parked in the carport.

I didn't want to leave, but as I looked back once more I realized I had seen too much and my view of Elvis was washed away by my grief. Jerry and I stayed by the ambulance until Joyce regained herself then we left through the back gate behind the church and found ourselves on the boulevard of broken dreams. There wasn't much for us to do, except offer our services in anyway that we could. Joyce and I went to the airport to pick up Kathy and some of the Stamps and it was difficult trying to negotiate a path through the fans that were lining up from Graceland to Forrest Hills Cemetery, three miles away. We didn't try to get through the front gates and instead pulled into the driveway behind the church next door that took us through the back gate up to the carport.

On the day of the funeral we were supposed to ride with Elvis' pilot, Milo High, to the cemetery, but somehow we got left behind, as we couldn't find his car, so we waited for them in front of Graceland. The streets were total chaos and traffic backed up for miles as people stopped in the middle of Elvis Presley Boulevard and got out of their cars. For as far as the eyes could see there was a sea of faces contorted with grief and signs declaring a love for him that would never die. Many times the procession ground to a halt for the safety of the fans that rushed onto the boulevard to touch his hearse and throw flowers in his path. A caravan of flower trucks preceded the cortege to the cemetery and the area around the mausoleum was engulfed in floral arrangements as Elvis was taken to a tomb twenty yards from his momma's grave, where he had visited only days before on the 19-year anniversary of her death. I was disappointed that they would not be side by side for eternity. I was glad that in a matter of weeks they would both be laid to rest beneath the green, green grass of Graceland.

After the funeral Joyce and I went with Ed Parker to get a bite, but no one had much to say - our unspoken pain was written across our faces. I also got a chance to visit with Kathy Westmoreland. She always had a deep loving bond with Elvis and the lovely girl with the beautiful high voice was devastated. I could tell that she would grieve for him for a very long time and I felt for her loss. Everyone began to reluctantly disband; we didn't want to leave, because when we did it meant that it was over; we knew the magnitude of this tragedy wouldn't hit home until we were back living our everyday lives without him. We held onto each other to feel closer to him and there we stayed until it was time for us to go...

In less than two weeks Ed Enoch called me and reasoned, "You know Elvis would be the first one to say that we need to get back to taking care of business." He wanted me to help The Stamps get a booking in a place they could fill. My heart wasn't in it and I just couldn't do it. Next I received a phone call from Dick Grob asking if I wanted to sell any of my negatives to my pictures or just my pictures. I didn't. My photos were mine, taken with love and care and excitement; they were the tangible part of my memory and I didn't want to share them until I was ready. Later others asked to use photos from my collection in their books, but I refused. Those books that trashed Elvis weren't going to be using my pictures no mater what they offered! I went though a denial period. I didn't want to see or hear anything about Elvis; I didn't even listen to any of his songs. He was gone. It was over; it was almost like it never happened.

But it did happen and it was the most extraordinary thing that ever occurred in my humble life; I couldn't cutout so much of my heart that had been dedicated to Elvis. As time went on I reached out again and discovered anew the depth of my love and admiration for who he was and how much he gave of himself and his vast talents... my feelings for him grow deeper and more precious every day and he will always be an important part of who I am.

It is amazing how many people believed in their heart that when Elvis died they lost a friend; even people who didn't know him had that sensation. Elvis touched many lives profoundly and he was personally involved with lots of people and had a connection or an association to so many others... then there were fringe acquaintances and people whose path he crossed, all of whom claimed a feeling of friendship for Elvis. In this book I have been forthright about my thread to the life of Elvis Presley and therefore you'll believe me when I say that he was my friend. I would have done anything he asked; given him whatever he needed and helped him however I could; without hesitation, I would have been there for him - in a flash! You can also believe me when I tell you that if a loved one of mine was dying and needed an operation or I was at the end of my rope and in dire straights, I would have gone to him and asked for his help, and knowing Elvis as we do you know that he would have done all he could for me and mine. I never imposed for anything more than an autograph, while many fans received jewels, cars, and articles of his costumes for the asking, so I knew that he was there for me if I was in trouble... that is the very definition of a friend.

Elvis' demise was tragic, but what has been done to his memory by the media has been equally painful. They write about his career as if he were a has been when he died, in spite of the facts to the contrary. An artist with songs and albums on the Top 40 Pop Charts, sold out concert tours across the nation playing to a world audience, and a television special, can hardly be seen as declining in popularity. At the time of his death, "Way Down," was Number One on the Country & Western Charts. With Country Music crossing over into the mainstream, like never before during that era, Elvis would've continued to grow in popularity, which is what happened anyway. After he passed away the album from his final tour went onto the Pop Charts around the world, his live single of "My Way/Can't Help Falling In Love," went Top 40 around the world, and even Ronnie McDowell's tribute, "The King Is Gone," went Top 40 around the world. His posthumous television special was Number One for the year in ratings, just like his appearances on Ed Sullivan were, just like his appearance on the Sinatra show was, just like his own singer special and the satellite broadcasts were. Since he died, every special or movie about him on television has always been Number One for the year. That's the way it is!

Even Elvis joked that when you'd come as far as he had there's only one-way to go, and that was right down the drain. But Elvis set the bar higher for himself with his intensity and exceeded his own wildest dreams and expectations a hundred times. In 1956 if anyone predicted that Elvis would be even more universally revered 20 years later, they'd have been laughed off - he was supposed to be a flash in the pan, a flavor of the month, a comet, a shooting star, the next Johnny Ray. From the moment he landed on top of the world, millions anxiously waited for him to crash and burn... they're still waiting. Many people were surprised that he made it out of 1956 still on the rise. He came back from the Army and beat the odds that were against him recapturing his past glory then soared to loftier heights than ever before with the greatest of ease. He came back from being the biggest star in Hollywood and did the television special that solidified his position as the most potent performer ever. He came back to the stage after eight years and picked right up where he left off as the most electrifying enter-tainer the world has ever known, and when he stood before the eyes of the world via satellite and poured his heart out in song, he etched his name in the firmament in forty languages as the most beloved artist that will ever live... he fell one comeback short; he couldn't get over the final hurdle within and though it ended his life it in no way diminishes the man or his career or the love of his fans.

I'LL REMEMBER YOU

In 1977 if someone said that decades after his death he'd be the most ritualized artist in history, it would've been hard to believe for even the most ardent fans. We worried then that there'd be no one around to tell the children about this amazing man. They wouldn't be able to see him live, to feel his magic, so how would they ever know? It added to our grief to think that he was gone and would soon be forgotten...what would it all mean if no one understood why thousands like me gave a part of their lives just to be near this man and experience the aura of this once-in-a-lifetime megastar? But like a true master, Elvis has continued to gain new audiences even in death and his position is affixed until the end of time and beyond. His virtual reality concert tour has challenged the gate of the top live stars of this era and his remixed singles and repackaged albums have topped the world charts; here in this new millennium he remains a relevant artist whose fan base is unmatched in expanse and range of age and culture - no other likeness has been more circulated and he remains the most identifiable person in the world. Not just his face; his image. From his turned up collar, curled lip, waterfall hairdo and sideburns, to his Pink Cadillac, jumpsuits, and Graceland, his persona is ingrained on our psyche - who do you think of when you hear about a fried peanut butter and banana sandwich?

He was an innovator, a true originator. Along with creating new musical genres, while wiping existing ones off the face of the earth, and setting all kinds of amazing records for sales of records and tickets and souvenirs, and commanding unprecedented audiences on television, and starting a social revolution in concert, he is a cultural touchstone to the modern artist. He is the father of the MTV video concept; his style of hair and dress in three different eras set trends that dominated the scene and are still in fashion; his session in the round during the "Comeback Special," is the first "unplugged" concert from a Rock Star; his format in the concert movies, of having cameras follow him around as he went through his routine, is what has become called, "Reality Programming." After Elvis, the time-honored trend of making singing stars into actors ended and the musical production movies with singing dialogue became extinct. Before Elvis there was no rebellious trend associated with singers; now in order to Rock you have to rebel. He was the first to travel encircled within an entourage and he's the only Rock star revered for his love of God and his momma.

His music not only crossed over Pop, R&B, Country, television, and movies, but also into Gospel. No one has reached a broader universal audience singing the word of God, and that would be his proudest accomplishment, no question. His biggest selling album to date is Elvis Sings The Wonderful World of Christmas. Who better to sing yuletide carols? He was the first artist to put a Rock & Roll song on the Pop Charts, and had some singles that went all the way up all three charts. He was the first artist to put a Gospel song onto the Top Ten of the Pop Charts and is the only artist to hit the Top Ten of the world's Pop Charts with Pop, Rock, Ballads, Country, Gospel, R&B, and Dance songs. He was the first performer to have hit singles from concert recordings and he has sold more live albums than anyone else.

He was so incredible that some expected him to be greater than he was... well how can you be greater than ELVIS PRESLEY? If he wasn't good enough than who is? Anyone who writes that this man's career has been anything but an unprecedented success that will never be rivaled, let alone surpassed, is ignoring the truth; anyone who dismisses the love of his dedicated fans, because of its intensity, is only revealing their shallow heart, and anyone that takes the position that Elvis' personal problems made him unworthy, is inhuman and cruel... these opinions are all worthless because they are based on the image of Elvis and not the man or the artist. He was a person as well as an entertainer; he was plagued with human failings, but more endowed with human kindnesses. How could we, who put him on that pedestal, expect him to stay there? We wanted him to be perfect because we were not; we wanted him to stay young so that we could hold onto our youth.

Elvis was justifiably proud of his career, he was impressed that he had come so far and was always astonished by the outpouring of love he received from fans around the world. He was a one-man empire, a powerful single entity who had experienced all the best that life had to offer and shared it with as many as he could. Elvis had remained true to his heart and never turned himself into someone else; he never thought that he was superior just because he was rich, because he had never felt inferior when he was poor. He lived by the code of conduct he had been instilled with during his upbringing and never felt that he had risen above being compassionate and considerate to those around him. His majestic talents were only matched by his boundless humanity.

Elvis has had an amazing career since August of 1977. It's often difficult to remember the glowing way that he was written about then after decades of reading about nothing but scandals, and fake love children, and sightings of him and his ghost. We have had to campaign to have his good name restored, and see to it that he is given his proper due. Some things never change, because the same powers that be that tried to run him out of the business, boycott him, censor him, and ban him, now strip him of the honors he that he earned and ignore his magnitude, while reaping the financial windfall that he creates and taking bows on his behalf. There has been no shortage of those who delight in chronicling Elvis' faults, but it is a well-known axiom, "If you cannot carve your place in history by virtue of your own talent, perhaps you can make it by being an assassin. There has been a mass media cottage industry built on bashing Elvis and the tragedy is that there has been such a market for it.

But the beauty of this story is that it has a happy ending... you see his detractors are officially out of ammunition. They have taken pot shots and cheap shots and struck low blows below the belt for thirty years, and still could not blast him out of the water or sink his fan support. The pundits and insiders have written and said every horrible thing that could ever be written and said about a person and Elvis is still universally beloved. Fortunately his fans are sophisticated enough to realize that there is a difference between a drug addict and a person addicted to pain medication and now their petty attacks on him have been rendered inert and irrelevant - a thousand books that aren't worth the paper they're written on are ready to be thrown onto the scrap heap and recycled into something worthwhile. Now all that is left to finally write about is how much we loved him, how supremely talented he was, how caring and devoted he was to his fans and to humanity, and how nobody will ever be a greater performer. He is the only force of nature that has not been diminished by death.

Elvis has launched still another comeback here in the new millennium; he is making new fans and reaching more people than ever. When the world grieved after the September 11, 2001 tragedies and turned to find music to pay tribute to the fallen and bask in our heritage, Elvis' inspired live performance of, "America The Beautiful," touched a chord and became his first Top Ten hit on the Pop Charts since 1972. Kids and teenyboppers discovered his music anew in the movie Lilo & Stitch and his old music found a brand new following. He became the first deceased artist to have a Number One album and single on the Pop Charts and the Dance Charts allover the world and the first deceased artist to go on a sold out worldwide virtual reality concert tour. He is the only artist that has been elected to the Rock & Roll, Country, and Gospel Halls of Fame, respectively. His image has been mainstreamed in commercials and movies and television shows, he sells more pictures and posters than any man ever, his name, face, and daughter can always be seen from the checkout stands, his movies are on the rise and his albums have no point of over saturation, because we can never get enough... any outtake, any alternate recording, or bootleg recording no matter what, even if it's just recordings of him clowning on stage or in private, we covet it as we would a piece of him; that's because he put his whole being into every moment of his career... a career that is still going strong...

I remember in the 1950s it was announced that Ricky Nelson

and Sal Mineo were getting more fan mail for a while than Elvis was; in the 1960s The Beatles were bigger than Elvis for a time, David Cassidy had more fan clubs in the early 1970s then their was the whole Disco era that led to the Michael Jackson, Madonna, Prince craze of the 1980s, and then the Metal, Grunge, Hip Hop world of the 1990s, which brings us to now, where now no entertainer sells more merchandise, has more fan clubs or comes close to having his cultural significance no matter who they kiss or what they expose on television. Between the tour of his home, his concert tour, and other shrines and museums he's still selling over a million tickets a year - not to mention how many people there are paying to watch impersonators recreate whatever small percentage they can of the inimitable musical legend. There have been all kind of flashes in the pan dubbed, "The next Elvis." His name is an adjective that means anyone who has unbelievable success in their field for any length of time. But the votes are in; there's never going to be anyone "Like Elvis," or "Elvis-like" and there will certainly not be another to challenge his crowning achievements. No generation will ever again become that attached to one performer, because of the complete saturation marketing of the industry. Today everyone has a favorite artist, back then we only had one - the one and only!

I was fortunate to have shared many moments of the life and career of this king among men from up close; we embraced and kissed and exchanged smiles and mementos and I was riveted by each encounter. I realized the significance of my relationship with Elvis was symbiotic, for as I stood there watching him perform on stage or saw him in his suite or was invited into the studio or to his home, even when I sat on his motorcycle with him, I was there as a representative of the millions who would never experience a personal interlude with him, never hear him in concert or get a kiss from him; this was the gift that he gave me to share with all of you and I feel blessed that a part of him will live on through me within the pages of this book.

Elvis often uttered a phrase that could serve as his personal epitaph when he would say, "Angels are able to fly to Heaven, because they take themselves so lightly." The declaration he made that best sums up his spiritual love and total commitment to his fans was, "As long as I live in this world, I solemnly sear to God that I will try to bring you joy and happiness with my singing." Once again he surpassed his own grandiose desire, because long after he is gone we continue to derive pleasure from the sound of his voice, we still thrill to the thrust of his hips and melt at the sight of his face. This isn't the end; it is only the beginning, as each generation will find love in their hearts for the man and the star that we lovingly call, "ELVIS! ELVIS! ELVIS!"

3 July 1973 - Atlanta - Vernon, Lisa, Linda Thompson

4 July 1973 - Atlanta Georgia Airport Hanger One. - From the
Archives of Sandi Pichon

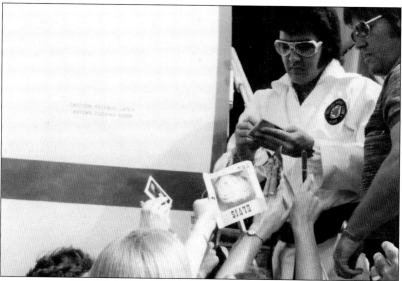

4 July 1973 - Atlanta Georgia Airport Hanger One. - From the
Archives of Sandi Pichon

162

4 July 1973 - Atlanta Georgia Airport Hanger One. - From the
Archives of Sandi Pichon

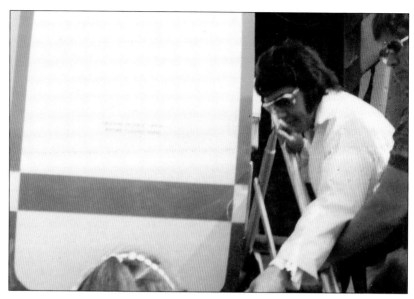

4 July 1973 - Atlanta, Georgia Hangar One - by Dorothy Campbell

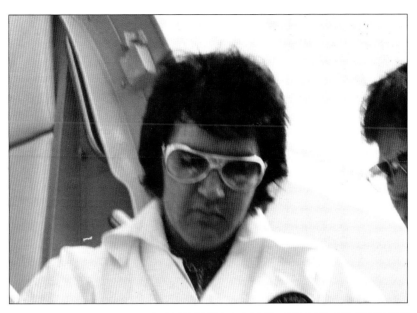

4 July 1973 - Atlanta, Georgia Hangar One - by Dorothy Campbell

27 August 1974 - Midnight Vegas

27 August 1974 - Midnight Vegas

27 August 1974 - Vegas Midnight

27 August 1974 - Vegas Midnight

1975 - Vegas, - Emilio Muscelli Hilton Maitre D'

29 March 1975 - Vegas Midnight

171

30 April 1975 - Atlanta Georgia

30 April 1975 - Atlanta Georgia

1 May 1975 - Atlanta, Georgia

1 May 1975 - Atlanta, Georgia - Dorothy Campbell

2 May 1975 - Atlanta, Georgia

2 May 1975 - Atlanta Georgia

2 May 1975 - Atlanta, Georgia

2 May 1975 - Atlanta, Georgia

2 May 1975 - Atlanta, Georgia

26 May 1975 - Dinner Vegas

181

25 April 1976 - Long Beach CA - Linda Strong

6 June 1976 - Atlanta GA, - Sandy Bryant, Me, Phyllis Tate.

182

6 June 1976 - Atlanta Georgia

6 June 1976 - Atlanta Georgia

6 June 1976 - Atlanta Georgia

6 June 1976 - Atlanta Georgia

6 June 1976 - Atlanta Georgia

6 June 1976 - Atlanta Georgia

31 August 1976 - Macon, Georgia - Felton Jarvis, Ed Hill

Taken on the set of
Loving You
Compliments of Carla Phillips

Taken on the set of
Loving You
Compliments of Carla Phillips

Thank You

For remembering me
during my illness

Elvis Presley

Peace On Earth

YOUR LOVE FOR ELVIS AND
HIS LOVE FOR YOU WILL
HELP KEEP THE LIGHT OF
CHRISTMAS SHINING ALL
YEAR THROUGH.

WE WISH YOU JOY & PEACE

VERNON AND THE COLONEL

The family of

Elvis Aron Presley
acknowledges with grateful
appreciation your kind expression
of sympathy.

Sandi

Your prayers and concern meant so much to Vernon during his illness and now are very comforting to the Presley family.

Thank you for your kind expression of sympathy. You have helped ease the burden of this most difficult time.

Sandy

from Sandy Miller Vernon's Girlfriend

Linda Thompson

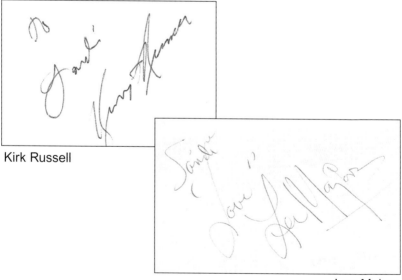

Kirk Russell

Lee Majors

Billy Swam

Righteous Bros

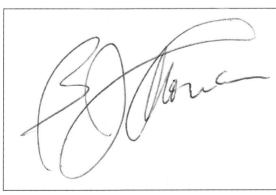

B.J. Thomas

195

Photo Credits

Joyce Hulsey, George Hill, Sean Shaver, Keith Alverson, Dorothy Campbell and Phyllis Tate were my friends who were kind enough to take pictures of me when I was at the stage with Elvis, and share these pictures with me. I am eternally grateful to them. Special thanks to Colleen Taylor for sharing her pictures and allowing me to use them. Also to Dorothy Campbell for the use of her Atlanta airport pictures.

Keith Alverson has a dynamite book ON STAGE, which contains some wonderful concert and candid shots of Elvis. Contact Keith at: **Eponstage@aol.com** or: PO Box 1666, Palmetto, GA 302268.

George Hill is another excellent photographer who sells his candid and stage pictures of Elvis. Contact George at: **RXAUB@aol.com** or: PO Box 15155, Panama City, FL 32406.

Sean Shaver may be contacted at: **seanshaver@hotmail.com**. Sean has penned several books, which may or may not be available. Sean was quite a presence on the Elvis scene and was privy to many backstage and personal visits with Elvis.

Sandi Haynes Pichon can be contacted by e-mail: **spichon@charter.net**